The Process of Reconciliation

John M. Hirsch

Copyright © 2012 by John M. Hirsch

The Process of Reconciliation
by John M. Hirsch

Printed in the United States of America

ISBN 9781619964013

All rights reserved solely by the author. The author guarantees all contents are original and do not infringe upon the legal rights of any other person or work. No part of this book may be reproduced in any form without the permission of the author. The views expressed in this book are not necessarily those of the publisher.

Unless otherwise indicated, Bible quotations are taken from The Holy Bible, New International Version®. Copyright © 1985 by The Zondervan Corporation. Used by permission; The Holy Bible, English Standard Version (ESV). Copyright © 2001 by Crossway Bibles, a division of Good News Publishers. Used by permission; The New Revised Standard Version (NRSV) Bible. Copyright © 1989 by the Division of Christian Education of the National Council of Churches of Christ in the United States of America. Used by permission.

www.xulonpress.com

Dedications

To Kathy, my wife of forty-three years, who patiently listened to me talk about this book over the years and encouraged me to continue writing.

To the hundreds of men and women of dozens of conflicted congregations who responded to questionnaires and allowed me to interview them and whose lives and stories influence the content of this book.

To the wonderful people of my first and only parish, Shepherd of the Lakes in Brighton, Michigan, who allowed me to grow up with them and who gave opportunity for my present ministry.

Acknowledgements

God and his passionate desire to reconcile the world to himself through his Son, and that those reconciled to him would be ambassadors of reconciliation to others.

Pastors Stanley Rock, Larry Foster, Peter Steinke, Bill Knippa and Jim Otte and many more pastors, colleagues and friends who provided encouragement and insights.

Garry and Nancy Goerdel who allowed me to use their cottage on the lake for organizing and writing much of this book.

Lynn Misch and Martha Jander who read, edited and gave advice in the writing and development of this manuscript.

Table of Contents

Introduction xi

Chapter 1 The Father with Two Sons 19

Chapter 2 A Look at Reconciliation 35
    A. God and People 39
    B. People and People 43
    C. Family Systems 47
    D. Reactions to Stress 56
    E. The Good News 59

Chapter 3 Helpful Personal Attributes 64
    A. Christ-Like Humble Attitude 66
    B. Transformed Heart and Mind 69
    C. Growing in Love and Obedience 75

Chapter 4 The Process 81
   A. Hindrances 83
   B. Moving Forward 87

Chapter 5 Understanding Values 111
   A. Personal Preferences 113
   B. Institutional/Well-Being 116
   C. Identity 117
   D. Lordship/Ultimate Purpose 125

Chapter 6 Getting to the Heart of the Matter 132
   A. Pray 134
   B. Mental Preparedness 136
   C. Build a Bridge 140
   D. Managing the Process 144
   E. Care-Listening 152

Chapter 7 Forgiveness 161

Chapter 8 Closing Thoughts 178

The Process of Reconciliation

Introduction

The phone call came from a friendly voice, which, despite its initial calmness, on this day began sharing a story of uncertainty and dismay. I had known this pastor for over a decade and he had grown and matured while serving three different churches in our state. On this day his concerns were both personal and professional. He wanted guidance in addressing a growing, and seemingly endless, string of issues that were permeating the life of the congregation he was now serving.

Though all congregations experience conflict from time to time, his congregation was in the throws of significant unrest. When he had come to this congregation five years previously, he followed a "charismatic" pastor who was both a personable and strong leader who had developed a staff-led ministry with intentions of growing the church to a much larger size. Despite his efforts this desire did not come to fruition. The church did not grow as anticipated and, in fact, slightly declined in both worship attendance and financial support. This pastor accepted a call to another congregation, and, after about a year of vacancy, the present pastor accepted the call to be the lead pastor.

With worship attendance and finances already declining, there was some recognition by the congregational leaders that the status quo could not be maintained. Some changes needed to be made. Under the new pastor's leadership, the congregation became more committee and task-force led. This move was to serve two purposes: cut costs and involve and engage more members in ministry planning and activities. Initially the transition seemed to be going well, but as decisions were made by leadership to go in this direction, communication about these changes to the whole congregation apparently broke down. Leaders claimed they were public about their decisions and actions, while some paid staff, who came on board with the former pastor, felt these decisions were made without their knowledge or input.

This breakdown in communication led one highly active, gifted and gregarious staff member to resign, but not gracefully. She had been a member of the congregation many years before being invited onto the staff and therefore had a large circle of friends. Upon her departure, her story, to some of her more closely-knit acquaintances, was that she was fired. The story of the leadership, who made the decision to move into a more committee/task-force form of leadership, was that she resigned of her own accord. As they saw it, they did not fire her. They felt they were engaging others in the ministry by taking from her some responsibilities she had assumed for herself, especially after the previous pastor left. To the leaders and new pastor, she was over-functioning, denying others the opportunity to serve. She saw this move by the leadership as sabotage of her ministry and an absence of appreciation for all the work she had done for the church over the years.

She and her family left the congregation but maintained relationships with many of her close friends who were still members. She frequently contacted this powerful and significant few, sharing her perspective of her leaving in an apparently emotional and convincing fashion. This led to an expanding circle of distrust of the congregational leaders.

To assuage the increasing tension in the congregation, the leaders tried a variety of formats to communicate "the truth" and keep the congregation informed and connected. In their own minds the leaders were doing what they could to keep the congregation focused and moving forward.

In spite of these efforts, the rumors, gossip and "speaking half-truths" continued. The end result was continued financial decline and more departures of "faithful members" who were primarily or secondarily connected to the original staff member. As more members left, pressure grew on the pastor and leaders to act. They held a congregational town meeting to explain, and hopefully clarify, the status of the congregation and the events that led to that situation. Again, despite these efforts, blame, fault finding, secret meetings and gossip continued to spread through the congregation like a virus run amuck. More staff people terminated their roles, adding fuel to the fires of discontent.

This internal conflict was exacerbated by the news that the well-liked part-time youth worker in the church, who was a full time counselor in a local public school, had been arrested and charged with inappropriate conduct with a youth at school. This information quickly became public information in both the community and congregation.

To alleviate any fear parents of church youth might have, the youth leader was immediately terminated, and a letter was sent from the pastor to the congregation clarifying the situation without placing the mantel of "guilty as charged" on the youth volunteer. The pastor wanted to speak the truth, as he knew it, while preserving integrity for himself, the congregation and the worker. On its own, this would have been a significant issue, but in the context of the events already in play, this fueled the displeasure and unrest in the congregation. There were more cries that the leaders were hiding something and that another worker had been inappropriately terminated. Distrust continued to spread.

In the context of this latest incident and its ensuing affect on the congregation, another emotion-laden event happened that cast another influencer into this already unsettled congregation. The son of the chairman of the congregation committed suicide. He was a well-known and well-liked young man. Layered over the division within the church, there was now a pall of grief and remorse. Emotions were pulled and tugged in many different directions as this event affected everyone regardless of their position on the other matters.

This tragic event added another factor to the rumor mill. As is often the case when young people take their own lives, people want to know details and the answer to the proverbial question, why? What caused this young man to "snap" and take his own life? What could have been done to prevent it? Did anyone see this coming? Was there anything on Twitter or his Facebook wall that hinted of this potential? There was a seeking for answers where answers were not to be found.

My conversation with the pastor ended with the decision that he would ask the leadership if it wanted to enter into a congregational assessment process that could potentially lead to reconciliation, health and a future with hope. In time, the leadership agreed.

The book that follows is the result of working for over twenty years with dozens of broken, fractured and conflicted congregations, not unlike the scenario above. Every story is different and every outcome is unique. Some congregations grow and mature through the process while others stay stuck and conflicted. Some move on to higher levels of ministry while others continue a slide downhill, perhaps hiring another consultant to "fix" what the last one could not or did not.

While congregations are spoken of as entities, they are really collections of unique individuals with various desires and capacities to move toward health. For congregations to change and move away from conflict, individuals within the congregations need to make intentional and proactive internal changes that lead to relationship change. A change in one person does not necessitate change in another, but if there is not change in one, there will not be change in another.

A key factor in a congregation, or any group for that matter, is that some people have a greater opportunity than others for influencing significant whole-life change in the organization. For example, in our opening story, because of her level of influence within the congregation, the first staff person to resign had one of the greatest opportunities to determine the congregation's future life. If she had moved into a behavioral posture of spiritual, emotional and cognitive health and had established some clear boundaries between herself and the congregation, life in the congregation would have been significantly different. Stress and tension would have been reduced and gaining a new vision and hope for the church would have been easier. The fault or blame for all of the congregation's problems cannot be placed on her shoulders alone as other members of the congregation enabled her to retain that much influence. Had they not listened she would have had little or no power.

The Process of Reconciliation

Chapter 1

The Father with Two Sons

From the summer of 1965 through the summer of 1966, I served as a volunteer at Riverside Lutheran Church, Detroit, Michigan, as part of the Prince of Peace Volunteers, a domestic inner-city ministry program of The Lutheran Church-Missouri Synod for college-age youth. Serving there during the Viet Nam War and just prior to the riots in Detroit in 1967 was a life-changing experience.

I worked with two gifted pastors. David Eberhard was a visionary with a lot of energy and determination. He embraced the diverse community and engaged many community leaders in a multi-faceted ministry that included a free medical clinic staffed by doctors, nurses, dentists and social workers, a home for "juvenile delinquent" boys, social work services and a resale store front. Lives of hundreds, if not thousands, of people were touched annually by these caring services.

Pastor Eberhard's associate, Joel Nickel, was a gifted artisan. He used his creative genius to develop a Vacation Bible School (VBS) program geared for inner-city youth. Using his own artwork of contemporary caricatures of Bible stories on long strips of butcher paper, he connected the lives of the Bible with the lives of the city.

To each teacher who assisted with VBS that year, he gave a signed copy of one of the pictures. As a teacher, I received a copy of *Home Again*, his rendering of the return of the prodigal son, the familiar story found in Luke, chapter 15. I had it framed, and it has hung on a wall in our home, wherever we have lived, for over forty years.

Though it will never have the fame of Rembrandt's painting, *Return of the Prodigal Son,* nor Henri J.M. Nouwen's wonderfully written reflection on Rembrandt's painting, *The Return of the Prodigal Son*, Joel's work grasps the depth of emotion that emanates from the process of a wastrel son returning into the arms of a loving father. Over the years of having this work of art in our house, it has become a significant symbol to me of the reconciliation process. (See picture at beginning of this chapter.)

Reconciliation is about relationship. It is about brokenness and the internal desire of humankind to be wanted and to have value. It is about the heart, the head and the viscera. It is about change, hope and a sense of future. It is about humility and honesty to self and others. It is about seeing the past through new eyes and the other person through a new lens. What once had meaning, no longer has meaning, and what did not have meaning, now does.

The story, as being told by Jesus in Luke 15:11-32, relates the interchange between a father and his two sons. One day the younger son saw fit to, in essence, declare his father dead and asked his father for his "share of the estate" (Lk.15:12). The father summarily divided his property between the two boys, giving, according to custom, the younger brother the smaller portion while preserving the larger portion for the older boy. The younger son took his possessions and, at the peak of a poor economy and a declining food supply, squandered them on self-indulgent behavior. To meet his needs for income and food, he took a job feeding pigs but soon realized that they ate better than he did. He was starving to death.

The Process of Reconciliation

At a moment of despair and extreme shame and guilt, the son realized that the servants in his father's house ate better than he did. Since it was he, and not anyone else, who had created the circumstances that led to his condition of bewilderment and defeat, he decided to humble himself before God and his father and in humility return home. He would seek his father's mercy, not to return as a son, but as a lowly servant. Though life was dreary and hunger consumed his nights and days, all was not lost. He had hope. He had hope that the father he had scornfully rejected would not treat him as poorly as he had treated him. He had new insights into life. It was less about him and his wants, and more about others and relationships.

His renewed thoughts motivated the son to return in the direction of his home. The father, who longed for this day and frequently scanned the horizon for his son's return, saw him at a distance and was filled with compassion. His "bowels" were churning within him and his emotions were stirred. He saw his son in poverty and lowliness and ran out to greet him with open arms. He put his arms around his son's neck and shoulders and embraced his filthy, stinky body. The rapacity of this lost, lonely and dejected son could not separate him from the father's love. The son's absence of merit or worthiness did not and could not overcome the overwhelming power manifested by the father's desire to embrace him and bring him back into the family.

The son confessed his sin and recognized his unworthiness. The father called for a celebration and adorned him with fine clothing and jewelry, while providing an exquisite banquet in his honor. Despite the son's willingness to work and live as a servant, the father embraced him as a full-fledged member of the family, with all the privileges of that position.

In short, this is a story about lives in which the intimate relationship between a parent and a child was fractured so deeply that it led to a total emotional and physical break. It is also a story about hope, love and new life. It is about having an abundant and fulfilling life. It is about seeing a future and having a future. It is about moving from existence to thriving. It is about reconciliation, but the outcome is not without cost.

When the story started, the younger son had little or no self-control. Emotional immaturity and a high desire for self-gratification governed his behavior. His life, his father's life and the relationship between the two of them was being sacrificed for material possessions and the pseudo life he thought they would bring. His view of life revolved around this narcissistic self, and it was spinning out of control without his awareness. He could not see that he could not see. He did not know that he did not know.

The son then came to the reality of the brokenness that resulted from his greedy behavior as well as a reality of what could be. His past painted a bleak picture of the future, but a transformed mind and a renewed spirit enabled a merciful disconnection from that past. The culmination of the reality of the wretched behavior that was leading to his death and a recollection of life in the family before his self-proclaimed freedom enabled him to see more clearly. He could now see what he could not see before, and he now knew what he did not know before.

The shackles of self-absorption and self-gratification were cut. Humility and the need to re-establish relationship enabled him to begin the journey back home. He acted on the new insight that eating as the poorest of his father's workers was better than starving while feeding swill to swine for someone else. Perhaps more significantly, he also recognized his sin (greed, selfish desires and wants, coveting, rejection of family and authority) and sought to make amends for the behavior that was destroying his life as well as his relationship with his father.

This parable does not describe the emotional state or reaction of the father when his son asked for his portion of the estate. From an earthly father's perspective, there was strong potential for feelings of hurt, anger, resentment, despair, disappointment or self-blame for not being a better father. After all, he had an older son who was faithful to his job and family; what happened with the younger one? What could he have done differently to prevent this from happening? How could his son treat him so cruelly after all he had done for him? How could his son take his future, walk out the door with it, and squander it on desires of the flesh? How could this son be so senseless? The potential for an emotional meltdown was great. If nothing else, he would have a heart made heavy by sorrow.

As the text does not describe the emotional state of the father, neither does it say how long the son was gone nor how much he squandered, but one could assume that it was not a short time, and it was no small amount of money. It was only after the money was gone, a severe famine had struck the whole country, and he was starving to death while feeding pigs, that the son "came to his senses" (Lk.15:17) and decided to return home.

At the same time, the father apparently never gave up hope for the son. The text notes, "While he was a long way off, his father saw him and was filled with compassion for him; he ran to his son, threw his arms around him and kissed him" (Lk.15:20). The father apparently had been searching the horizon faithfully on a regular, if not daily, basis for any glimpse of his son's return. The father's insides, his *gut*, yearned to see his son. When he saw him "while he was a long way off" (Lk.15:20), he immediately ran out and greeted him with a strong fatherly embrace. He was uncontrolled in his ability to wait for his son to make it all the way home. While the son was still mentally rehearsing his story of contrition and unfaithfulness, he was being surrounded with acceptance, love and forgiveness. He was experiencing grace and mercy the likes of which he never anticipated.

The rehearsed message still came out, and the sinner confessed his sin to God and his father. He was genuinely contrite while recognizing that the most he could hope for was to be called *slave*. The concept of being a *son* in the family again was now a foreign thought. However, he had hope. It was not founded on his own merits or the thought that his

The Process of Reconciliation

father would be overjoyed to have his "lost" son return, but on genuine humility and a desire to be a servant in the house of the one who had shown him love and modeled integrity.

He was now seeing life and the world through a different lens. He realized he was not the center of the universe, and everything did not revolve around him and his wants. The new view was not about the past, but rather the present and the future. It was about others and his relationship with them. It was about a humble attitude and renewal of mind. It was about being responsible and having integrity that flowed from a transformed heart. This new perspective of life was about boundaries, self-management, and self-control. It was about letting go and moving on. This new assessment of self was about love and a deeper understanding of that word.

There was a blessing to the father as well. He was able to move on. He did not chastise, blame, criticize, scold or shame his son. He did not express any self-blame or make any apologies for what he might have done differently to prevent this separation in the first place. He would not allow the past to determine the present or future. Instead, he was present in the moment and immediately initiated a celebration event. He called for the best robe (a festival garment as a mark of dignity not to be worn while working) to be put on his son's shoulders, a ring (symbol of authority) to be put on his finger and sandals (not worn by slaves, but by sons) to be put on his feet. A fatted calf was slaughtered and the eating and celebration began "for the son of mine was dead and is alive again; he was lost and is found" (Lk.15:24).

Reconciliation resulted when both the father and the son viewed the incident that broke their relationship through a different perspective than the one used when the event happened. The son lost all sense of arrogance. Humbleness now overshadowed self-aggrandizement. Respectfully, he came to his father with a broken and contrite heart. He no longer saw himself as being in total control, but now realized he had been out of control and needed the affirmation and support of his truly wiser and more understanding father.

The father, who could have chastised his son for being so foolish and squandering his life, chose instead to manifest the fullness of his fatherliness in mercy and forgiveness. His role and position were not diminished or diluted but were fully manifested through an emotional and physical embrace of his son. The deep, heartfelt love he had for his son could not be contained. In the blink of an eye not only had the playing field been leveled but the son was put on a pedestal. A healthy relationship had been re-established or restored.

Integrity, trust and honesty were now established components of their new life together.

Reconciliation was the process and the product of what happened. Jesus told this story to give insight into the kingdom of God. It only had value because it reflected real-life events. In this case, it was brokenness in relationships. For healing to take place, the younger son had to realize that brokenness existed. His culpability needed to be acknowledged. He also needed a sense of hope and a desire to re-establish relationship, even at a modest level. A new attitude needed to emerge, toward self and his father. An action plan needed to be developed and made operational. Not only could the son do wise thinking but he also had to do wise acting.

The father needed to be vigilant and hopeful as well. He needed to stay focused on the desired outcome of having a healthy relationship established. He needed to be a good listener and have an understanding heart for a contrite person. He needed to base his behavior on the core of who he was and his desired outcome, not on the behavior of a son who in his youth rebelled against him. The father did not forget the past, but he did not let the past delimit the present or future.

The contributions of both parties, not just one, led to the reconciliation. Without both, it never would have happened. The focus of this book builds on that foundational understanding of reconciliation. Partial or temporary reconciliation can take place if one party makes some changes toward health, but for lasting reconciliation to take place, changes in both are essential.

Reflections on Chapter 1

Luke 15:11-32 The Father with Two Sons

1. Read through the story of the father with two sons three or more times, savoring the words that are there while striving not to interject your own thoughts or opinions on what the text is saying.

2. List three positive attributes of each of the three characters in this story.

Younger son:

1. _____
2. _____
3. _____

Older son:

1. _____
2. _____
3. _____

Father:

1. _____
2. _____
3. _____

3. With which of the three people in the story do you most identify? Why?

_____

_____

_____

4. There was stress in this family.

What did the younger son contribute to it? _____

_____

What did the older son contribute to it? _____

_____

What did the father contribute to it? _____

_____

5. At the moment of greatest tension or discord in the family,

What was the younger son doing? _____

_____

What was the older son doing? _____

_____

What was the father doing? _____

_____

6. Ultimately, there was some reduction in the discord.
What did the younger son do to help this happen? _____

What did the older son do to help this happen? _____

What did the father do to help this happen? _____

7. In viewing this parable as a story of three possible broken relationships (father and younger son; father and older son; older son and younger son) that experienced reconciliation in one of those relationships (father and younger son),
What could the father and only the father do to bring about reconciliation?_____

What could the younger son and only the younger son do to bring about reconciliation?_____

What could the older son have done to bring about reconciliation?_____

8. Many Bible scholars see Jesus using the father role as a descriptor of his heavenly Father and each of the sons as representing two different aspects of relating with him, one of pride and self-aggrandizement while the other of humility and repentance. With that model in mind, as we work on reconciliation with others, how should we first approach the Father? What will be his response to us?

_____
_____
_____

Chapter 2

A Look at Reconciliation

The tongue that brings healing is a tree of life, but a deceitful tongue crushes the spirit. Prov. 15:4

Leave your gift there in front of the altar. First go and be reconciled to your brother; then come and offer your gift. Mt. 5:24

Reconciliation is a process of restoring or healing a broken relationship. It recognizes that any relationship between two or more people is fluid, unstable and subject to emotional, mental, physical and spiritual highs and lows. As a dynamic and living system, it is inevitable that at some time a relationship will become stressed and strained, if not fractured and even broken. This is an unavoidable reality.

Differing or conflicting goals, beliefs, attitudes, opinions, perceptions, values, interests or needs may lead to any number of reactive responses. The brokenness may be obvious and openly acknowledged when people attack or consciously avoid someone else. For example, two men who were angry at each other were shopping in the same big box store. One saw the other before the other saw him. In one scenario, he rapidly moved down the isle toward the other and then verbally attacked him for what had been said in a totally different setting. In another scenario, rather than risking encountering him, he left the store without buying what he had come there to buy.

Broken relationships may develop over time and not be discerned until there is so much hurt and/or resentment that a minor incident may trigger a major reaction. For example, a volunteer youth worker came to church on a Sunday morning and as usual joyfully greeted the youth gathered for his class. Without warning, he abruptly changed posture and tone of voice, read a letter of resignation and walked out of the church without any further explanation.

Everyone involved was stunned and shocked and wondered what caused this behavior. Unknown to many, tensions in this volunteer had been building for many years due to gossip and rumor. Congregational members who did not like the current pastor convinced the volunteer that this pastor was trying to get rid of him by subtly sabotaging his ministry. He listened to these people. Seeing this as an affront to his integrity, he chose to dramatically end his ministry with an abrupt cut off. Rather than seeking to determine the veracity of the stories by directly talking to the pastor, he allowed others to do his thinking. He emotionally reacted and thereby undermined his ministry with the youth and his integrity with some church members.

Conflict may come "out of the blue." For example, when one person overhears a conversation in which a "best friend" makes slanderous remarks about that person to another person, emotions become overwhelming and a fissure forms in the relationship. A completely new attitude toward that person develops. Feelings of hurt, anger, resentment or alienation, or some combination of all of them, may be experienced. Mental and emotional wrestling with what to do with this new information may confound these feelings. Should this new information be overlooked or denied? Should the person pretend not to have heard it? Should the speaker be confronted? Will the slandered person go to a friend and share a story about how hateful that other person was (gossip)? Increased division or eventual concord will depend upon how all parties involved in the relationship decide to respond.

Reconciliation is the intentional course of action engaging two or more people in an emotional, mental, relational and spiritual process of restoring health or of creating healing, harmony or concord to a relationship that is fractured or broken. As a process, reconciliation takes time and assumes that all parties involved seek to conciliate. It assumes that there is motivation that flows either from wanting to reduce one's own pain or from desiring to establish a healthier, more pleasant relationship with the other person, or both. It also assumes there are resources, internal or external, natural or supernatural, that enable or assist in achieving the desired outcome.

All people are unique in their own right. However, in relationships there are overlaying forces that influence how they function as a unit or group. To bring about the reconciliation process, it is important to understand these ubiquitous, but not always obvious, factors influencing all relationships.

A. God and People

As a matter of priority, the relationship between God and people needs to be addressed first. In the Christian community, it is acknowledged that the relationship between God and his prime creation is not only bruised and strained but also broken. The fall into sin by Adam and Eve is not a one-time event but a prime force that has created havoc for all people since. Wars and battles between nations, countries, tribes, families and family members have been a common occurrence since our first parents were ushered out of the garden. We may desire and crave peace, especially peace that will last, but our sinful self will not allow it either with our neighbor or God.

People do not and cannot live in a harmonious relationship with God by their own choosing. As much as they may desire to do so, there is nothing they can do to reconstruct and rebuild the relationship that existed between God and his creation before the fall. The now imperfect cannot choose to do that which is necessary to restore health and resolve differences with the Creator. They may wishfully seek to justify or rationalize behavior that separates them from God with the hope that good behavior will overcome any division. The seeking and the desire may be there, but the ability and resources to accomplish unilateral restoration are beyond the sinful human's capacities.

Therefore, if restoration or the state of being reconciled is to be achieved between the Creator and the humans he created, it has to come from the Creator. God's initial action of reconciliation in the Garden of Eden was a unilateral and unconditional act of love to restore wholeness to the relationship that was broken when the ultimate joy of his creation decided to play God. In so doing, men and women found out what it was like to be in God's disfavor, though not rejected. There was no shame in nakedness before their act of defiance, but now Adam and Eve were experiencing it. This new feeling led to the desire to hide. The desire to hide led to creating clothes of fig leaves, a form of protection that would not last.

Recognizing their new knowledge of good and evil and the futileness of making clothing out of fig leaves, God called them to task and held them accountable for their behavior. He also demonstrated grace and showed his love for them by making clothing for them from skins of animals (Gen. 3:21). He gave them protection that would last. Metaphorically, this sacrificing of life and the shedding of blood was a foretaste of a future redemptive act that would not last just a long time, but forever.

The apostle Paul in the New Testament succinctly wrote, "But when the time had fully come, God sent his Son, born of a woman, born under law, to redeem those under law, that we might receive the full rights of sons" (Gal. 4:4-5). This coming of the Christ and his living, teaching, modeling, praying, healing, engaging, confronting, suffering, being ridiculed, being abandoned, dying, rising and ascending paid the price not only so that we would not have to, but because we could not. It was God "reconciling the world to himself in Christ, not counting men's sins against them" (2 Cor. 5:19).

This act of reconciliation by the Father through the Son enables the state of reconciliation we now have with him as we live in him. The apostle Paul celebrated this Good News with the new Christians in Rome when he wrote, "This righteousness from God comes through faith in Jesus Christ to all who believe. There is no difference, for all have sinned and fall short of the glory of God, and are justified freely by his grace through the redemption that came by Christ Jesus" (Rom. 3:22-24).

It was this Good News that led Paul also to express excitement about life and relationships in their growing Christian community in Corinth when he wrote in about A.D. 55:

> So from now on we regard no one from a worldly point of view. Though we once regarded Christ in this way, we do so no longer. Therefore, if anyone is in Christ, he is a new creation; the old has gone, the new has come! All this is from God, who reconciled us to himself through Christ and gave us the ministry of reconciliation: that God was reconciling the world to himself in Christ, not counting men's sins against them. And he has committed to us the message of reconciliation. We are therefore Christ's ambassadors, as though God were making his appeal through us. We implore you on Christ's behalf: Be reconciled to God. God made him who had no sin to be sin for us, so that in him we might become the righteousness of God (2 Cor. 5:16-21).

The Christians in Corinth were to see each other differently than they had before. Because of their relationship with God through Christ by the power of the Holy Spirit, they were to see each other from a new view of life. As they now had a new life with God, they were to have a new life with each other. If they were to claim Jesus as their Lord and Savior, they were to live lives that reflected that new belief. If they were to say the Great Reconciler was their God, then reconciliation was not only something that happened *to* them but also was something that happened *through* them. Not only were they recipients of this love but they were to live it through sharing it with others. The demonstration that they were reconciled to God would come not only by believing but also by living renewed and transformed lives in relationship with others.

B. People and People

As we are enabled to live in a *set-free* (redeemed) relationship with God through Christ, we are enabled by grace through faith to live in a set-free relationship with others. This is especially true with others who also believe in him as Lord and Savior, i.e., the household of faith. Moreover, just as the relationship between God and people was critically wounded by the actions of the people, so are the relationships between people and people. In fact, the brokenness between and among people may be more difficult to reconcile, as all parties contribute to the brokenness. In the brokenness between God and people, only one side broke and continues to break the relationship. In interpersonal relationships, both parties can and do contribute to the brokenness. It is a condition of humanity that there will be conflict and discord. We cannot choose not to have it.

1. Sin

There are many factors that lead to the brokenness of relationship between people, not the least of which is the situation of our birth. As the psalmist wrote, "Surely I was sinful at birth, sinful from the time my mother conceived me" (Ps. 51:5). Paul reiterated this condition of humankind when he wrote, "As it is written: 'There is no one righteous, not even one; there is no one who understands, no one who seeks God. All have turned away, they have together become worthless; there is no one who does good, not even one'" (Rom. 3:10-12). James, the brother of Jesus, wrote, "What causes fights and quarrels among you? Don't they come from your desires that battle within you?" (Ja. 4:1). All of us are sinful by nature and therefore cannot, even as much as we would desire to do so, live in total harmony with all people. It just cannot happen.

Sin is our inherent inability to be complete as God is complete. It is our *missing the mark* of having the capacity to fulfill the greatest of all commands: "You shall love the Lord your God with all your heart, and with all your soul, and with all your strength, and with all your mind; and your neighbor as yourself" (Lk. 10:27 NRSV). Sin is an inherent aspect of who we are if we are alive. It is not a character flaw, a personality defect, or a psychological syndrome that can be resolved by counseling or medication. It is of the essence of being human. People are by nature sinful, and because of that sinful nature, they do sinful things.

All sins are not equally weighted in the eyes of society, but all sins separate people from God. Taking a pencil from the office supply store without paying for it is not seen by society as being as heinous as the actions of the terrorists who crashed the planes into the World Trade Center twin towers in New York City on September 11, 2001. However, in the eyes of God, both sins separate people from him.

Likewise, as God forgives the stealing of a pencil when the sin is genuinely acknowledged and confessed, so are the sins forgiven of a mass murderer. As Peter said, "I now realize that God does not show favoritism, but accepts men from every nation who fear him and do what is right" (Acts 10:34). God is no respecter of people. He treats them all the same, loves them all the same and, when they publicly acknowledge him by word and deed as their Savior and Lord, forgives them all the same. Because of his Son's obedience upon the cross, he sees people through different eyes, and now he guides his people to do the same, as his ambassadors of reconciliation.

2. Other factors

Though sin is the universal underlying factor of all broken relationships, other factors contribute to conflict and relationship breaking as well. We are all complex individuals, each having and being a unique self. There is no one else just like us, and despite the fact that we may say to another when something traumatic happens, "I know how you feel," we really do not, nor can we. There are just too many variables that differentiate us from others. These include, but are not limited to:

- Gender and gender roles
- Birth order position, gender sequence and length of time between births
- Physical, mental and emotional differences (genes)
- Deaths of siblings or parents
- Adoptions into the family
- Birth order position of the parents
- Relationship between parents
- One parent being a "critical" parent
- Blending of two or more families due to remarriage after death or divorce
- Ethnic and cultural diversity in customs

- Mores and values
- Mental illness
- Strains of physical illness
- Spiritual health
- Natural and human created disaster

C. Family Systems

Along with the attributes or factors that make us unique and different from all others, we are part of a still bigger picture. We are not alone in this world. We come from families and families are a part of a given society. We are influenced by our families and the society in which that family exists. We create subgroups that we call nations or tribes while also dividing ourselves into families, clubs, teams, associations, fellowships, organizations, guilds, committees and other social and relational networks. We might be members or participants in many of these at one time, changing roles and relationships accordingly. Even these roles and relationships are not static. As time passes and participants change, relationships change. Stress or tension may increase or decrease, depending on who is in the club and who may or may not be present at any given time or event.

Observers of these societal relationships have noted that along with the obvious and overt factors that influence relationships, there are other significant covert influencers. These are the forces of being in a system. A system is a "placing together" or arrangement of things into an organic whole. As such, no person is independent unto himself. No person is truly an island. All components are connected and interconnected such that as one influences another, the other is changed. At the same time, this change brings about change in the original influencer. In one influencing another, neither is the same as before. This dynamic has been referred to as an *emotional system.*

As used here, the term *emotional* is not used to refer to our *feelings* as it usually does in the vernacular. It is a reference to automatic physiological reactions that take place in all living organisms, especially those with a brain. Feelings, as we normally use the word, are what we experience when we become conscious of the physiological reactions. We *feel* upset, hurt, angry, resentful, joyful, excited, calm, agitated, peaceful, etc., as a result of some deeper interpersonal factors influencing our relationships.

We see this dynamic of automatic physiological reactions played out in our culture. We read or hear stories of individuals who are accosted by another individual on a public street with a large number of people present, and no one takes action to stop it. Intuitively, and individually, those involved know someone should do something. Someone should stop it, but no one does. No one tries to intervene. No one even uses a cell phone to call the police. The reaction is basically to be immobilized. People are frozen into inaction. All are caught up in a system that is influencing their feelings and their behavior. As one does not act, another does not act. No one tells the others not to act; they just do not. The automatic forces of the system are more powerful than what each individual knows or thinks should be done. These forces are so strong that they overpower the knowledge of knowing that a person needs help. These are automatic physiological reactions that come from deep within the brain.

Similar actions can take place in organizations like churches, school boards and civic clubs. Individuals are given positions of authority, e.g., chairperson of the congregation or treasurer, and do not serve well in those positions. Many members of the organization seem to know this, and it may be fodder for gossip and rumor, but no one acts upon that information. Each time there is an election, the individual is reelected, and each time people complain about the individual's poor performance in that position. The system is a strong influencer of behavior, and continued poor performance is enabled by the system.

Significant for us to understand what is happening in the street event, a church, club or civic organization is being aware of the role anxiety plays in all relationships. While anxiety is identified with many different labels (anger, resentment, frustration, excitement, anticipation, exaltation), it is more beneficial to think of it in the broader picture of being an intense emotion. Again, this intense emotion is not what we call feelings but an automatic physiological reaction. This is not just psychological or sociological but a biological response of an individual and those in the system.

By its very nature, anxiety travels between and among individuals in a group. It is infectious. This is seen in the herding effect of one startled cow influencing the behavior of the whole herd or one person yawning in a board meeting and others following suit shortly thereafter. One person's laughter can lead others to laugh.

Where the anxiety travels defines the limits of the emotional system. The startled cow in the nearby pasture does not influence the herd of cattle down the road in another pasture nor does a yawning or laughing person in a board meeting influence another person in another room down the hall. Though manifested in significantly different ways, anxiety influenced the behaviors of both cattle and people, but only to the limits of their sphere of connectivity and influence.

Since the role of anxiety is important in understanding the emotional system, we will take a closer look at two significant aspects of it.

1. Chronic anxiety

In family-systems thinking, the force identified as anxiety is refracted into two subgroups, *chronic* and *acute* anxiety. The former comes from any perceived or real stressors that we encounter over a lengthy period of time and is often beyond our awareness, e.g., caring for a chronically ill parent, spouse or child; experiencing prolonged unemployment or prolonged employment in a vocation that is emotionally demeaning or draining; or having to commute daily to work in a major metropolitan city. Chronic anxiety may develop by living in a family exhibiting lengthy emotional, physical, verbal, sexual or substance abuse. It may include being regularly exposed to media (news and talk show programs on radio or TV, DVDs, music, movies, newspapers, magazines, the internet and social networking sources like

Twitter and Facebook and all the good and evil they have to offer) or significant people in our lives who influence our thinking, values, beliefs, attitudes, opinions and behavior.

Chronic anxiety may be subtle and easily overlooked, denied or dismissed. It becomes so much a part of the homeostasis or balance of our lives that we do not recognize the effect it is having on us. It may not show significantly on the emotional radar screen, but it is continually there, influencing, if not gradually eroding away, the underpinnings of our emotional, physical, spiritual and relational health.

Because of the financial meltdown in America and around the world in 2008−2009, we may say that watching the value of our savings and retirement programs diminish significantly does not affect us. We tell ourselves that every time in the past when the stock market has gone down, it has come back again. Therefore, it will come back again. However, the constant input of the vicissitudes of the stock market over an extended period may still put us *on edge* and increase the possibility of knee-jerk reactivity, physically or verbally, to a relatively innocuous stimulus, e.g., shouting at or physically striking a two-year-old for playing with the food on his dinner plate.

2. Acute anxiety

Acute anxiety is the product of abrupt and unexpected stimuli that trigger spikes of anxiety that diminish in a relatively short time. This reactive response generally occurs to real or perceived threats and is experienced for a limited duration. However, it can act as an igniting event that inflames conflict that has been smoldering for some time. Some examples are:

- The "teaching" event of a pastor that led a parishioner to react strongly against him when the parishioner saw it as ridicule and the pastor saw it as spiritual discipline
- A temporary loss of job that led to a marital conflict over the spending of money
- Sending out a haughty and condemning email to many of your church friends because someone in the church "offended" you
- Working late when you were to take your spouse out for a birthday dinner

While chronic anxiety is not always in the awareness of the person having it, acute anxiety is. It happens when an emotional sensation in the body is recorded in the brain as a feeling. Attempts may be made to overlook it, but the somatic reaction is not easily dismissed. A chemical change has taken place. Adrenalin or epinephrine is secreted from the medulla (inner cells) of the adrenal gland that is about the size of a lima bean, sitting on top of the kidney. The hormone epinephrine increases the heartbeat and blood pressure and gives the urge to freeze, flee or fight.

I was writing this portion of this book while staying at a summer cottage of a friend. I had been there before, but this was the first day and first evening after not being there in a number of months. As I was sitting at night alone at the kitchen table, typing into my laptop computer, I had grown accustomed to the air conditioner coming on and going off. Outside of that noise, and the whirring of the ceiling fan above my head, it was very quiet. You could almost feel the stillness.

Now, while I was writing this, the refrigerator behind me "kicked on," and I felt a rather sudden and unexpected startle effect in my whole body. I felt my muscles in my shoulders and upper back immediately become tense, and my brain instantaneously increased the acuity of my ears. For the few tenths of a second before I realized it was the refrigerator turning on, there was a sense of vulnerability and a bit of fear. Was I really not alone? Was someone else in the cottage? Was someone trying to break in? Was I in danger? The mind thought all kinds of things, and the body lost its degree of comfort. Upon realizing that it was the refrigerator turning on, the sense of vulnerability and fear dissipated quickly, and my heartbeat returned to its resting pace, but this experience gave me a very clear and personal example of acute anxiety affecting my system.

3. Uncontrollable factors

As we look at all the factors that contribute to conflict and tension between people, we see that we have very little control over many of them. The sin piece is in all of us, and that will be discussed later. We have no control over our gender, birth order, birth order of our parents, a death in the family, having an adopted brother or sister, or being in a blended family due to death or divorce and remarriage. We cannot change our ethnicity, nor do we feel we have much control over the local, national or world events that affect our lives.

Whether we were in New York City on September 11, 2001, or 2,824 miles away in Los Angeles, the destruction of the twin towers of the World Trade Center changed our lives.

Whether or not we had stocks in our portfolio, the financial crisis of 2008—2009 affected all of us, directly or vicariously through others. We had no control over those events or the increased chronic anxiety that has been added to the western world, if not the whole world.

Since September 11, 2001, we have seen many countries in North Africa and the Mid-East in political and civil unrest and civil war. Régimes are under siege. Some leaders have resigned, and others are being challenged or killed. The European Union is being challenged from within. Some countries are on the brink of financial collapse. Our own country is struggling under a massive debt load, and political dissension seems to be commonplace.

D. Reactions (Not Response) to Stress

With so many factors that influence our relationships with others being out of our control, we could easily rationalize any conflict or brokenness in relationships by saying, "That's life, what's the use of trying to fix anything? I can't change them and they can't change me." Such thinking can lead to relatively unproductive behavior called emotional *cutoff*. Cutoff is a process of separation, isolation, or withdrawal. It is a form of running away or denying the importance of significant relationships and is an extreme method of distancing oneself from others.

In emotional cutoff people consciously or unconsciously strive to disallow others to influence their thinking or behavior. They ignore, avoid or minimize any contact with others. Emotional barriers are built, and energy is spent in denying the existence or presence of the other person. Emotionally sensitive issues may be avoided or denied. For example, an individual may physically:

- Leave a marriage (separation, divorce)
- Leave a company (quits and/or finds a job elsewhere)
- Leave a church (leaves that congregation for another of the same denomination, of another denomination, of another religion, or drops out of that religious belief system altogether)
- Leave any other organization or group (football team, choir, debate team, ex-students association, Hells Angels, etc.)
- Make excuses for not attending a family event that often happens at Thanksgiving, Christmas, Easter, or other religious or national holidays

Physical cutoff reflects the emotional significance another person, or persons, are having on our lives. Though we may strive to be free through not being physically present at a meeting or family gathering, the significant influencer may not be our own sense of healthy self-autonomy. Instead, it may be our way of avoiding pain, hurt, conflict or tension. In other words, we are not free. We tell ourselves that we are, but in reality we are allowing the presence of the other person to determine our behavior. We paint a picture in our head about what the event will be like if we go, and we do not like the picture. Therefore, in order not to experience the created picture, we choose to avoid the event.

Furthermore, we do not see other options of what could happen if we do go, nor do we see what we contribute to the conflict or tension. We tend to paint the picture from a cause-effect mentality and not as an emotional system. We see it as "I go to the event. They cause me pain or hurt. I don't want to feel pain or hurt; therefore, I will not go." We do not see it as a relationship into which each person brings his own *stuff*, and that stuff influences and is influenced by the stuff of the other. We also tend not to see how the stuff of all the others at the event can influence the relationship between the two of us. It is really difficult to see the bigger picture and how the interaction of all participants in the event influence and are influenced by the behavior of all the others.

Paradoxically, when we intentionally avoid others, we are actually "fused" into the other person by granting that person power to determine what we do or do not do. Though we may not be consciously aware of it, we are saying to the other, "I am giving you power to determine my behavior. I am allowing past experiences to determine my present and future behavior. I am allowing your stuff to determine my sense of self." The avoidance is not from a position of *being okay* or neutral, but from a position of fear and elevated anxiety. The greater the resistance to the other person, the greater is the power that person exercises over us. In other words, the more we struggle to be free, the more we put ourselves into bondage.

E. The Good News

Not all of life and relationships are futile. We are not automatically caught in a spiraling-down system in which there is no hope. There is good news and there is Good News. *First*, God has already reconciled each one of us to himself through his Son, Jesus Christ. Therefore, the breach in the relationship between God and people is no longer an issue for those who believe and trust in him as Savior and Lord. God has taken care of that. He has reconciled the world unto himself.

Second, since this healing has taken place through the work of the Spirit who dwells within believers, he has given the church the ministry of reconciliation, and, as such, we are ambassadors for Christ (2 Cor. 5:20). We are empowered by "a Spirit of power, of love and of self-discipline" (2 Tim. 1:7).

Third, in giving us this ministry, God equips and empowers us through a variety of resources, including Scripture and his Spirit, to carry out this ministry. God has revealed himself in his Word and therefore gives us tools and information essential for the reconciliation process.

Fourth, since reconciliation, as a process, is to lead to a desired outcome that is different from the current condition, it calls for a mindset different from the one that led to the conflict. It calls for a renewed and transformed change in our thoughts, attitude, feelings and behavior toward the other person. It calls for visualizing a different and more blessed future and moving toward it.

As the apostle Paul wrote while addressing this subject, "So from now on we regard no one from a worldly point of view. Though we once regarded Christ in this way, we do so no longer. Therefore, if anyone is in Christ, he is a new creation; the old has gone, the new has come!" (2 Cor. 5:16-17). We are to approach the process from a *new creation* perspective.

Though this is the desire, this is not always reality. All parties of a dispute or broken relationship, even those within the church or a household of faith, are not always "on the same page at the same time." All may not desire to reconcile, or, even if they do, they may not be at the same level of emotional and spiritual maturity. Although this may militate against the desired outcome, it does not necessarily prevent it from ever happening.

We can only manage ourselves and not the other person. What we do and what we say, as well as how we do it and how we say it, may make the difference as to whether or not the state of being reconciled is the final result. Therefore, keeping these Good News factors alive in our thinking and behavior means that the outcome may be even healthier and more wholesome than before the reconciliation process began. The behavior of one individual can significantly affect the outcome of the process in a positive direction. The attributes of that person will be considered next.

Reflections on Chapter 2

1. Identify a time when you were in conflict with another person. What was the conflict about? _____
_____

2. What was the outcome of this event?_____
_____

3. If the matter of dispute was <u>not</u> reconciled, what do you think you contributed to this outcome? _____
_____

4. If the matter of dispute was reconciled, what do you think you contributed to this outcome? _____
_____

5. Regardless of the outcome, were there any Scriptural passages that came to your mind that influenced your behavior? _____ If so, even if you don't remember book, chapter and verse, what were those words? _____
_____

The Process of Reconciliation

6. Paul wrote to the church in Corinth that they were "Christ's ambassadors." Since we read those words as applying to our lives today, what do those words mean to you, and how do they influence your behavior? _____

_____

_____

7. Now that you have some awareness of an "emotional system," share an example when you saw the influence of this process at work in your life. _____

_____

8. Give an example of chronic anxiety in your life and share how it has affected you. _____

_____

9. Give an example of acute anxiety in your life and share how it affected you. _____

_____

10. Who is the person you can influence the most in bringing reconciliation to a broken relationship? _____

Chapter 3

Helpful Personal Attributes

If then there is any encouragement in Christ, any consolation from love, any sharing in the Spirit, any compassion and sympathy, make my joy complete: be of the same mind, having the same love, being in full accord and of one mind. Do nothing from selfish ambition or conceit, but in humility regard others as better than yourselves. Let each of you look not to your own interests, but to the interests of others. Let the same mind be in you that was in Christ Jesus, who, though he was in the form of God, did not regard equality with God as something to be exploited, but emptied himself, taking the form of a slave, being born in human likeness. And being found in human form, he humbled himself and became obedient to the point of death —even death on a cross. Phil. 2:1-8

Reconciliation is not a process entered into lightly and without much thought. Since it involves restoring and renewing relationships, not just solving problems, it engages our whole self, not just our analytical, problem-solving capacities. It is wise, therefore, to enter into it as well prepared as possible. If the desire is truly to encounter the other in a way that reduces tension, stress and disharmony, then attentive thoughtfulness must be given to the right sense of *self* needed to help bring about the desired outcome.

While there are many attributes essential to this purpose, Scripture sums it up in these three:

- A Christ-like humble attitude
- A transformed heart and mind
- A growing in obedience and love

These are like the legs of a three-legged stool. You need all three to have balance. One leg is better than no legs as it raises the seat up and establishes a place to sit, but it does not have stability. Two legs are better than one as the second leg adds another force for stability by preventing wobble in some directions, but the stool will still fall without a third force. All three legs are needed. Only then will the stool stand on its own accord. Only then will it serve the purpose for which it is intended without assistance from other forces.

It can be moved. It can be painted. Many different people can sit on it, but it will still be stable in its own right.

This is also true for the reconciliation process. Even if all the right techniques and steps are known and implemented but there is no significant change in the attitudes and hearts of the people involved *before* the process begins, the process will be significantly handicapped. In fact, it may never happen at all. The reconciliation process is not just doing the right thing; it is doing the right thing with the right spirit. It is not about winning or losing but about keeping "the unity of the Spirit through the bond of peace" (Eph. 4:3) and having more life and hope than either person had before the process began. Therefore, before a person begins to engage in a process of intentionally moving a relationship toward wellness, that person needs to begin the process of moving toward a healthier spiritual life.

A. Christ-Like Humble Attitude

To help us manage, regulate and control ourselves as we enter into and work through the reconciliation process, Scripture lists a number of attributes that are essential here and in all of life. *First*, we are to have a Christ-like, humble attitude (Phil.2:1-11). The human ego is a strong and powerful force. It often wants to dominate our lives and, when push comes to shove, wants to win. In its own pervasive way, the ego wants to come out on top. It may be motivated by a fear of failure or a desire to win. In its seeking for significance and purpose for life, it may regress to a variety of thoughts and behaviors that seek to advance self at the expense of others.

Guilt or shame due to a public or private sin that has not yet been internally resolved can play havoc in our lives. Gender, age, birth order, death, divorce, and the other factors listed in "Other Factors" above feed into who we are and how we see ourselves. We can let them overwhelm us and strip us of any sense of worth, or we can let them give us a sense of self-imposed aggrandizement and superiority. We can feel unworthy of help, or we can feel we do not need it. We can capitulate to everyone's wishes, or be guarded and defensive and do nothing for anyone. We can over function and try to manage every job that comes our way or under function and become involved in nothing. None of these behaviors serves the purpose of reconciliation.

Therefore, Jesus said we are to give them up and set aside this focus on self-gratification and self-exoneration and take on a new self and a new role, the role of servant. "Then he

[Jesus] said to them all: 'If anyone would come after me, he must deny himself and take up his cross daily and follow me. For whoever wants to save his life will lose it, but whoever loses his life for me will save it. What good is it for a man to gain the whole world, and yet lose or forfeit his very self?'" (Lk. 9:23-25).

This is a Spirit-driven, voluntary giving up the focus of *what's in it for me* to a focus on others through the eyes of Christ. This is not a thinking less of self, but a thinking of self less. It is a reframing of one's own life by looking through a different lens.

This change is like the difference between viewing a Magic Eye picture before you understand how to focus your eyes so as to see the 3-D view in the picture and afterward. There is a world of difference. Before you understand how it works, the picture may look like rows of repeating figures in a variety of colors with no apparent meaning at all. After you learn how to *look through* the obvious surface picture, a whole new panoramic picture comes into view. It is almost impossible to believe that underlying what is on the surface is something very spectacular. That which was blurry, muddled and had no meaning is now clear and vivid. There is an *ah-ha* that reflects seeing what was untenable before.

The changed attitude we are to take on is like this new unimaginable picture. It is fresh and alive. This new view of seeing oneself is about seeing the other as a fellow citizen in God's kingdom who is loved just as we are loved. It is about believing the petitions in the Lord's Prayer where we say, "hallowed be your name, your kingdom come, your will be done on earth as in heaven" (Mt. 6:9-10). It is about letting go of the old and taking on the new. It is about life, hope and freedom, freedom from the past and hope for the future. It is about seeing the other through a new lens, a lens not of this world but of Christ's world. It is about becoming free in Christ. After all, "It is for freedom that Christ has set us free" (Gal. 5:1).

B. Transformed Heart and Mind

Second, we are to have transformed and renewed hearts and minds. The author of Psalm 119 notes in verse 2 that they are blessed "who keep his statues and seek him with all their hearts" and later reflects on the same theme when he writes in verse 112, "My heart is set on keeping your decrees to the very end." Moving into the New Testament, Jesus summarizes the whole law in these words: "Love the Lord your God with all your heart and with all your soul and with all your mind.

This is the first and greatest commandment. And the second is like it: Love your neighbor as yourself. All the Law and the Prophets hang on these two commandments"(Mt. 22:37-39). In writing about Paul's second missionary journey while he was in the city of Philippi, Luke writes, "One of those listening was a woman named Lydia, a dealer in purple cloth from the city of Thyatira, who was a worshiper of God. The Lord opened her heart to respond to Paul's message" (Acts 16:14). Then in his letter to the Roman churches, Paul wrote, "Do not conform any longer to the pattern of this world; but be transformed by the renewing of your mind"(Rom.12:2).

As compared to being stubborn, inflexible, and resistive to the will of God and the process of health and wholeness, we are to be outfitted with new thinking that embraces new feelings and a new spirit. Paradoxically, we are to move from being in a position of perceived total control to that of being without control and a slave or servant of Christ. Such an attitude change is manifested in an emotional, relational, behavioral, cognitive and spiritual transformation of one's own being.

A significant event or encounter with God in the context of his Word may trigger this process. We see that happening in Saul's conversion experience on the road to Damascus

(Acts 9:1-16). Paul, then named Saul, had received permission from the high priest to go to Damascus to search out, hunt down and bring as prisoners to Jerusalem any men or women who were followers of the Way. As he traveled, he experienced a sudden flash of light that caused him to fall to the ground. He then heard a voice say to him, "'Saul, Saul, why do you persecute me?' He responded, 'Who are you, Lord?' The voice replied, 'I am Jesus, whom you are persecuting. Get up and go into the city and you will be told what you must do'" (Acts 9:4-6).

Saul was speechless, and now blind, but obeyed the voice and with the aid of those with him went into Damascus. There he encountered a man named Ananias who also had received a vision from the Lord. Initially, Ananias was reluctant to follow the Lord's command to meet with Saul as Ananias was a believer in Christ and was very aware of Saul's reputation as a Christian hater. The Lord assured Ananias that he had selected Saul to "carry my name before the Gentiles" (Acts 9:15). Ananias obeyed. He went to the house where Saul was staying, entered, placed his hands on Saul and stated that he was there at the command of the Lord so that Saul "may see again and be filled with the Holy Spirit" (Acts 9:17b). With this, "something like scales fell from Saul's eyes and he could see again. He got up and was baptized" (Acts 9:18). "At once he began to preach in the synagogues that Jesus is the Son of God" (Acts 9:20).

On the other hand, a transformed heart and mind may come as the result of a life-long spiritual upbringing through parents and grandparents. Timothy was such a person. Spiritually influenced by his mother (Eunice) and grandmother (Lois), he was spiritually led in his early life to be servant/shepherd/leader in God's kingdom work (2 Tim. 1:3-7).

Another example of the beginning of this transformational process is found in the first chapter of the Gospel of John. The setting is the preaching of John the Baptist and his paving the way for the coming of the Lord (Jn. 1:19-34). John then writes:

> The next day John (the Baptist) was there again with two of his disciples. When he saw Jesus passing by, he said, "Look, the Lamb of God!" When the two disciples heard him say this, they followed Jesus. Turning around, Jesus saw them following and asked, "What do you want?" They said, "Rabbi (which means Teacher), where are you staying?" "Come, he replied, "and you will see." So they went and saw where he was staying, and spent that day with him. It was about the tenth hour. Andrew, Simon Peter's brother, was one of the two who heard what John had said and who had followed Jesus. The first thing Andrew did was to find his brother Simon and

tell him, "We have found the Messiah" (that is, the Christ). And he brought him to Jesus (Jn. 1:35-42a).

In this brief vignette, Andrew, who had been a disciple or follower of John the Baptist was introduced to Jesus by the Baptizer. The curiosity of Andrew and the other disciple of John led them to follow Jesus. They entered into a rather lengthy dialogue with him that lasted the greater part of a day. Whatever transpired in this discussion was transformational in Andrew's life. He was no longer the same. He began to see life through a new perspective. There was new thinking and spiritual insight: "We have found the Messiah (that is, the Christ)" (Jn. 1:41). It affected his whole person, his thoughts, his emotions and his behavior. "The first thing Andrew did was to find his brother Simon and tell him" (Jn. 1:41). It strengthened the relationship with his brother: "And he brought him to Jesus" (Jn. 1:42b).

When Simon came to Jesus, Jesus "looked at him and said, 'You are Simon son of John. You will be called Cephas' (which when translated, is Peter)" (Jn. 1:42). With these words, Simon, now called Peter, began a completely new journey in his own life. He remained a fisherman of fish, but more importantly, he became a fisherman of people for the kingdom of God.

Peter now had a new mental image of what is truly important and significant in life. It led him through some emotional and spiritual high peaks and some deep valleys. His highs included experiencing the transfiguration of Christ upon the mountain (Mk. 9:2-8) and boldly professing that Jesus was "the Christ, the Son of the living God" (Mt. 16:16). His lows involved an attempt to stand in the way of Jesus' fulfilling his role as Savior, to which Jesus rebuked him by saying, "Get behind me, Satan! You are a stumbling block to me; you do not have in mind the things of God, but the things of men" (Mt. 16:23).

This new relationship with Christ also included perhaps the darkest moments of Peter's life when he denied Jesus three times right before his crucifixion, just as Jesus said he would (Lk. 22:54-62). Therefore, Peter's spiritual journey went about as high as one can experience on this side of heaven and as low as anyone could imagine, but all of these experiences together empowered him to write, "prepare your *minds* for action; be self-controlled; set your hope fully on the grace given you when Jesus Christ is revealed" (1 Pt. 1:13) (emphasis added).

Peter acknowledged that the journey of a believer in Christ is long and sometimes rough and challenging, but there is reason to stay the course. There is reason to have hope, and that reason is the grace of the revealed and revealing Christ. This grace enables and empowers self-control that prepares our minds for healthy thinking and healthy behavior. It enables us to relate with others through transformed hearts and minds and provides a foundational piece for the process of reconciliation.

C. Growing in Love and Obedience

Third, there is a need to be growing in our love and obedience to God. As servanthood springs from a transformed and renewed mind, so do love and obedience. Jesus said this clearly to the expert in the law who challenged him with the question, "Teacher, which is the greatest commandment in the Law?" (Mt. 22:36). He replied, "'Love the Lord your God with all your heart and with all your soul and with all your mind.' This is the first and greatest commandment. And the second is like it: 'Love your neighbor as yourself.' All the Law and the Prophets hang on these two commandments" (Mt. 22:37-40).

The expert in the law was looking for a way to justify himself and his legalistic attitude. He was trying to find fault with Jesus and his lifestyle of preaching, teaching and living that welcomed *sinners* and forgave them, healed the sick, fed the hungry, gave sight to the blind, gave mobility to the lame and calmed storms. In response, Jesus clarified that obedience to words alone was not being a follower of God or keeping his Law. Instead, the words had to flow out of a person who was "born again" (Jn. 3:7), someone who was now different because of belief in the Son and someone who has eternal life. The Father has enabled and the Spirit has transformed this life into being disciple, servant, and follower. This person has been transformed in all aspects through a relationship with the living God filled with love, grace and mercy.

This love does not originate with the believer, but with the Father, who ultimately manifested this love through sending his Son into the world of humanity to redeem it from its brokenness and sin. It is through trusting in the Son that this love is grasped and returned to the Father, by loving him and others. Loving and obeying are not a theology of the head, as the expert in the law posited, but a theology of the heart, as Jesus so clearly stated. It is not about only one dimension of being human, the head; it is also about the center, the very core of our whole being, the heart: body, mind and spirit. Love and obedience are about whom we love. They are about our will, our desires, our passions, our fears, our perceptions, our genuine self. They are about a heart that has been softened. They are about being loved into loving. They are about experiencing grace into living grace. They are about being forgiven into forgiving.

In response to this gift of life and love from the Father, John noted that our behavior needs to be guided by our transformed hearts when he wrote, "We know that we have come to know him if we obey his commands. The man who says, 'I know him,' but does not do what he commands is a liar, and the truth is not in him. But if anyone obeys his word, God's love is truly made complete in him" (1 Jn. 2:3-5). He goes on to state, "let us not love with words and tongue but with actions and in truth" (1 Jn. 3:18). The transformed heart leads to a life of obedience.

In summary, a different person, a humble person who is in the process of being spiritually and personally transformed and renewed, needs to come to the reconciliation table. Thoughts of winning and losing are to be abandoned. Getting *their just dues* or a *pound of flesh* is anathema. Seeking revenge and making the other person pay are prohibited.

Instead, a spirit that exemplifies the fruit of the Spirit, i.e., love, joy, peace, patience, kindness, goodness, faithfulness, gentleness and self-control (Gal. 5:22-23a), is welcome. After all, "Against such things there is no law" (Gal. 5:23b). A more managed and controlled self needs to approach the reconciliation process than the one who initially contributed to the brokenness in the relationship.

As with the prodigal son, a transformed and renewed mind along with a humble heart and a contrite spirit are foundational components of the reconciliation process. They are the basis upon which any words said or actions taken gain value and reflect integrity. Without them, all the right techniques, lofty goals and well-constructed plans and actions are of no value.

Reflections on Chapter 3

1. List the three essential legs of the reconciliation stool:

   a. _____

   b. _____

   c. _____

2. How does one grow to have a more Christ-like attitude? _____

3. Share a major event, or many "smaller" events, that have been significant in the spiritual transformation of your heart and mind. _____

4. Share a time when you felt unconditional love from another. _____

5. Share a time when you believe you were showing unconditional love toward another, whether or not they knew it.

_____
_____
_____

Chapter 4

The Process

Do not let any unwholesome talk come out of your mouths, but only what is helpful for building others up according to their needs, that it may benefit those who listen. And do not grieve the Holy Spirit of God, with whom you were sealed for the day of redemption. Get rid of all bitterness, rage and anger, brawling and slander, along with every form of malice. Be kind and compassionate to one another, forgiving each other, just as in Christ God forgave you. Eph. 4:29-32

"If your brother sins against you, go and show him his fault, just between the two of you. If he listens to you, you have won your brother over. But if he will not listen, take one or two others along, so that 'every matter may be established by the testimony of two or three witnesses.' If he refuses to listen to them, tell it to the church; and if he refuses to listen even to the church, treat him as you would a pagan or a tax collector." Mt. 18:15-17

Though people may want broken or bruised relationships healed, they are often reluctant to enter into an intentional process to bring about reconciliation. This is true between people who love and care for each other, as well as people who desire to never see each other again. Perhaps we can rationalize not making efforts to reconcile with people we do not plan to see again, but with others, e.g., spouse, neighbor, sibling, fellow church member or a fellow worker, it is more difficult. We may feel in our gut some necessity to patch things up, but that does not mean we will actually do something to bring it about.

Just knowing a relationship is broken and that reconciliation is needed for a healthier relationship does not automatically motivate either person to do anything about it. We may just let something eat at us, hate what is happening, and yet not do anything to change the situation. We may have attacked another person verbally or physically, or have been attacked by them, and know that *the Christian thing to do* or the right thing to do is to address the matter with them one-on-one. Yet, we take no steps in that direction. We may even go so far as to deny the brokenness exists or that we are emotionally hurting. Though the actual reasons for this failure to act are multi-causal, there are a number of fears that may play significant roles. These fears may be trivial to some, but to others they create enough anxiety to disallow any efforts to seek reconciliation.

A. Hindrances to Getting Started
1. Not knowing what to say

First, we may fear not knowing what to say or how to say it. With little experience and no formal training in the mechanics of one-on-one addressing of personal issues, we may feel ill equipped or unprepared to engage in the process. The resulting anxiety may immobilize us and cloud any thinking of potential positive outcomes. The Good News, that we have been reconciled to God through Christ's atoning sacrifice and that he has empowered us for the ministry of reconciliation, is lost in the blur of anxious negative reactivity. We feel ill equipped and focus on what we do not know or think we do not know. Our fear is that if we do not know what to say, we will say something wrong and botch the whole process. The relationship may be in worse shape after the encounter than it was before.

2. Thinking that the other person will not listen

Second, we may fear that the other person will not listen. We fear that the other person will be indifferent or insensitive to our needs, hurts, concerns or emotions. The fear can be that we will be transparent and share from the heart our hurts and concerns, but the other person will not listen. Consequently, we will be less of a person than we were before.

To justify not acting, we may say things like, "He just does not like to talk about things," or "he is a nice enough person, but he just does not listen." We may see the other person as one who changes the subject or physically or emotionally moves away from us when we try to address what we see as a conflict that needs to be resolved. We do not see the other person as a person who is bitter or angry, but as one who gets irritated or stubborn and refuses to discuss the matter if we push toward having a frank conversation.

3. Leave it alone; it is not as bad as it seems

Third, we can rationalize that things are not really too bad, and if the matter is addressed, it will only stir things up, like hitting a wasp nest full of wasps with a stick. To prevent the possibility that things may get worse, we do nothing. We continue to fret or regret, but take no action. We do not want to "rock the boat" with the hope that if we say or do nothing, the boat will not sink but stay afloat and actually stay on course.

This deliberate or inadvertent inattention to the issue helps maintain a sense of homeostasis or balance in the system. The relationship may not be healthy or functioning well, but it is perceived as better than it would be if this matter were brought out into the open. In essence, we do not want to risk moving from dis-ease or discomfort to health as it may result in disaster. So rather than risking any change, even change that may improve relationships, nothing is done in the hopes that doing nothing will prevent making things worse.

4. I will lose

Fourth, we may fear losing. Reconciliation is seen as a win-lose proposition, and if we engage in it, we will lose. We may see ourselves as inadequate or inferior to the other person, and regardless of how well we might handle the process, we would still *come out on the short end of the stick.* If we do not have a healthy sense of who we are and know our boundaries, we may allow the other person to intimidate or disparage us, even if that person has a strong desire to reconcile. We suffer from an absence of worthiness or fortitude that would allow us to address the issues to the best of our abilities and then be okay with the outcome. The internal fear of losing prevents any external movement toward reconciliation.

This fear is reinforced when 1) we have this fear along with the fear that the other person only plays to win, 2) the other person would deny the existence of a conflict, or 3) the other person denies participation in the conflict.

5. The other person is unapproachable

Fifth, we may intuitively know that some people like to win at all costs, and to try to reconcile with them would be very difficult. The fear is that the other person would have to admit to contributing to the brokenness, and the other person would never do that. In fact, if the person is in a position of authority or power, there may be *heck to pay*. Any suggestion or inference to that person being a part of the problem would lead to us being marginalized and fired, if it is in a business, and disciplined if it is in a church. Reconciliation could never take place, and the person who brought up the matter would be made to feel worthless or foolish for even broaching the subject.

In such a relationship, the focus shifts from addressing the relationship between *us*, to *me* and what *I* did wrong. That which was intended to be addressed and hopefully reconciled through a process guided by love, care and good listening is seen as an attack or threat.

Consequently, we are to be put in our place, set straight or even told that it was the devil or evil that led us to suggest there was a problem. We are not embraced or welcomed for having the desire to reconcile, but humiliated or shamed for putting the other person into a position of dealing with an issue that has been deemed insignificant. It is like speaking to a brick wall, or worse yet, having the brick wall fall on us. After the conversation, we feel awful, evil, stupid, disrespected or unworthy. The thought is, if talking to the other person will hurt me, why would I even try to reconcile in the first place?

B. Moving Forward

Having noted many reasons for not engaging in a reconciliation process, there still are many reasons to do so. God encourages us to do so. Along with bearing the fruit of the Spirit, love, joy, peace, patience, kindness, goodness, faithfulness, gentleness and self-control, God includes the ministry of reconciliation in the life of a Christian. It is not optional behavior for those who say they follow the voice of the Good Shepherd (2 Cor. 5:11-21; Jn.10:14). Though there may be reluctance to do so, we are to be intentional about entering into the process. To help us get started, Paul encouraged "the faithful in Christ Jesus" with these words:

> As a prisoner for the Lord, then, I urge you to live a life worthy of the calling you have received. Be completely humble and gentle; be patient, bearing with one another in love. Make every effort to keep the unity of the Spirit through the bond of peace. There is one body and one Spirit— just as you were called to one hope when you were called—one Lord, one faith, one baptism; one God and Father of all, who is over all and through all and in all (Eph. 4:1-6).

Here Paul encourages the believers to "make every effort to keep the unity of the Spirit through the bond of peace"(Eph. 4:3). We are not to remain complacent or stuck with the status quo when the status quo is maintaining and sustaining conflict and strained relations in the church, home or work place. Instead, we are to move out of this stuck and unproductive mode into the ministry of reconciliation. God realizes that as long as there are bruised, wounded and broken relationships in the body of Christ, it is not functioning well and consequently is not fulfilling the Great Commission to "go and make disciples of all nations" (Mt. 28:19).

Persistent unresolved conflict leaves members of the body wounded and bleeding emotionally and spiritually. In some aspects of their lives, they remain bound to the past and, consequently, are not free to move on with life. Joy may be depleted and hope is snuffed out. Sustained and enabled conflict provides a poor witness to those not in the body of Christ of what life in a healthy body is like. It empowers the devil to continue to work on all parties and wreak havoc on the relationship and individual lives. It is a lose-lose situation for all involved.

To move the reconciliation process forward, there are some steps an individual can take to prepare for this intentional action. These steps help develop the sense of self-control, self-discipline and self-regulation that are instrumental in achieving a desired outcome. They help a person reduce the affects of anxiety upon themselves by being more responsive and less reactive in the upcoming interaction. The steps enable one to be more objective and less subjective. They help one stay in the conversation while not being consumed by it. They help one focus on principles and process and not on blaming and faultfinding. They help level the playing field by disallowing or reducing some of the fears noted above in the section on reasons why someone might not enter into a reconciliation process.

1. Know who you are and whose you are

Inasmuch as we may be people who have been sinned against or are experiencing emotional and spiritual pain over the behavior of another, we are at the same time redeemed saints of God. Jesus paid the price of his life for us so that we would be his "friend" (Lk. 5:20) in whom he would reveal all that the Father revealed to him. We are also "heirs" of the kingdom (Gal. 4:7) in which all that he has will also be ours. Jesus was very transparent in his revelation and held back nothing in expressing his love for us, including indwelling us with the Holy Spirit. Consequently, we are empowered, enabled and encouraged to engage in the process of reconciliation.

While empowering, enabling and encouraging, God is not guaranteeing the outcome that we desire, or if so, not necessarily on our timeline. We may desire to meet with a person one time, and when the conversation ends, all matters and issues of conflict will be resolved, and we will go away as good friends. This may happen, but this may be more the exception than the rule. In reality, because we are rational, emotional, spiritual and relational beings, we often need time to process things, and the time allotted to the conversation may not be enough.

There may be a need for a number of conversations. We may need time to discuss the matter with another trusted friend to help us understand what we are contributing to the conflict as well as to help us understand the way the other party may see the issue. We may need time for the Holy Spirit to work in us through the Word, confession and absolution, the Lord's Supper, prayer, devotional material, meditation, sermons, friends and any other process he wants to use to change our hearts and renew our minds. Consequently, the outcome may be *more* than we imagined, not just what we had in mind.

As noted above, many factors influence and affect the outcome of any interchange between people, not the least of which is the sinfulness of all parties involved. This cannot be denied, but acknowledging it helps provide perspective of our sinfulness as well as God's unbounding grace, mercy and forgiveness. Though it is not always easy to be obedient to the loving Lord and let his way and be ours, Scripture states, "Cast all your anxiety on him, because he cares for you" (1 Pt. 5:7 NRSV).

Elsewhere, Paul wrote to the churches in Rome, "In all things God works for the good of those who love him, who have been called according to his purpose" (Rom. 8:28). Jesus encourages us to pray (Mk. 11:24). His brother James affirms the Lord's thoughts with the injunction to pray to God, without doubting, and God can and will provide the wisdom needed to act boldly and with courage (Ja.1:5-8). Paul underscores these thoughts with, "So whether you eat or drink or whatever you do, do it all for the glory of God"(1 Cor.10:31).

2. Do a "self" assessment

For some, the thought of engaging in a reconciliation process may not actually start with the desire to reconcile but with the desire to prove the other person is wrong or at fault. The objective is to set things straight by correcting or rebuking the other. The goal is winning, with losing not an option. The only desired outcome is for the other party to see the error of their ways and in so doing grant victory to us.

The reality is that in a reconciliation process neither party can approach it from a win-lose position. That is a position of superiority and self-righteousness and is counter-productive to the process. It violates the values established above: humility, servanthood, transformation of the mind and spirit undergirded by love and obedience. Starting with what we know, i.e., that there is some unrest, dis-ease, angst, turmoil or unsettledness between the parties in the disagreement means that the parties need to start the process by doing self-assessments of what they are contributing to the problem. The starting point is not looking for the fault in the other but looking inwardly to internal sources that disallow us from dismissing, forgiving or overlooking this matter.

Jesus helps us do this with this parable:

> Can a blind person guide a blind person? Will not both fall into a pit? A disciple is not above the teacher, but everyone who is fully qualified will be like the teacher. Why do you see the speck in your neighbor's eye, but do not notice the log in your own eye? Or how can you say to your neighbor, 'Friend, let me take out the speck in your eye,' when you yourself do not see the log in your own eye? You hypocrite, first take the log out of your own eye, and then you will see clearly to take the speck out of your neighbor's eye (Lk. 6:39 NRSV).

Jesus is directing us to take a self-assessment of our own motives. Are we blinded by rage or anger? Are we hanging onto issues from the past that for some reason bind us to the past? Are we saying to ourselves that the other party should come to us first because the other party offended us? Are we mountain climbing over a molehill and in so doing making this more than it really is? Are we a rescuer who wants to solve this problem at any cost and yet do not see our contribution to the issue? Are we bossy, pushy or abrasive in our usual dealings with people, and regardless of what we say, it comes out as an attack on the other? Are we harboring a sin we have committed that has not been confessed and absolved and is now being projected onto the other? Are we intentionally or unintentionally discrediting the other by giving them labels like "stupid jerk," "hard headed" or "impossible to deal with"? Are we displacing, or striving to give to another, some judgment that justly should be ours? Are we condemning another for that which is so prevalent in our own life? These may be hard questions to answer, but they need to be answered.

The plank in our own eye may be obvious to us. It may be obvious to others. On the other hand, it maybe obvious to others, but not to us as it comes out of the shadowside of our personalities. This shadow side is not inherently evil or sinister, but a side of us that is molded and shaped by all the

The Process of Reconciliation

factors listed earlier that help make us who we are. They are powerful forces in determining our behavior, but we do not see them. For example, we may be quick to speak and slow to listen, just like our father. We may be unaware of this, and yet it has a profound affect on how we treat others and how they see us. We may think we are good listeners, but others see us as one who has all the answers before they even finish the question. There can be big planks.

Regardless of the cause of this blindness, Paul wrote in his epistle to the Philippians:

> "Your attitude should be the same as that of Christ Jesus: Who, being in very nature God, did not consider equality with God something to be grasped, but made himself nothing, taking the very nature of a servant, being made in human likeness. And being found in appearance as a man, he humbled himself and became obedient to death—even death on a cross!" (Phil. 2:5-8).

We are to humble ourselves and seek to remove any known and unknown obstacles that hinder the reconciliation process. We need to approach the process *in good faith* with a desire that the process is not hindered by what we do or say, or any negative thoughts or attitudes toward the other.

The reconciliation process is entered into through a contrite heart that has done an honest assessment of self, seeking to discern what about us would be getting in the way of our being a redeeming force in this process. It might even call for seeking the input from a trusted person (friend, confidant, pastor, counselor, etc.) who could give honest feedback as to what they see in us that might hinder a redemptive and healing process. It may be that we are so blinded by seeing the issue through our own eyes for so long that we do not and cannot realize there may be another way of looking at this issue. Another person, who is not a stakeholder in the outcome of the process, may be able to provide a more objective assessment of us. This self-assessment piece of taking the log out of our own eye before striving to take the speck out of another person's eye is key to any reconciliation process. The process cannot be successful if this step is neglected.

3. Put God first

The desire is that God shall be glorified and that his will shall be lived out within us, between us, and among us. Action is based on what God wants to happen in this process, not what we want or what we think the other wants. This is taking a position that is defined by principles and values governed by these words: "You shall love the Lord your God with all your heart, and with all your soul, and with all your strength, and with all your mind; and your neighbor as yourself" (Lk. 10:27 NRSV). Out of honor, respect and a healthy fear of God, the desire is to address a conflicted relationship with another person with the same passion of redemptive love that the Father lived out with us through his Son and continues to live out with us through the Holy Spirit. As Oswald Chambers noted, "You must be so pure in your motives that God Almighty can see nothing to censure." [1]

4. Get a perspective

One old saw warns us, "don't go off half cocked." Another notes, "don't be a loose cannon" shooting everywhere with no clear purpose in mind. Another adage admonishes us to "get our ducks lined up" before we start to do a project. The idea is that before we initiate any task or mission, we need to have an understanding what that mission is and have thought through what we plan to do. There is a need to have the appropriate resources available at the right time to fulfill the project in a timely fashion. In other words, if there is a desire to be reconciled with another person, we should do our homework and become spiritually and emo-

The Process of Reconciliation

tionally prepared before we enter the reconciliation process. We should start with knowing who we are and whose we are. We should understand our position, needs, interests and our desired outcome. We should understand the presenting problem and its significance for us that led to the brokenness.

Recently I played golf with a friend of mine. We started early in the day and were not playing with anyone else. It was a nice day and we were enjoying ourselves. Things were going okay, and I hit a fairly long drive off the tee on a long par three. Its trajectory appeared to take it somewhere in the fairway, though neither of us could see exactly where. My friend's shot was not as long and had a slight slice. Since his ball was closer, he played his ball next, and then we began to look for mine. While in the search, we saw a ball in the fairway in approximately the location we thought mine might have been. I took a club, addressed the ball, and after doing what I usually do before hitting the ball, I stroked it somewhat toward the green.

Shortly after I struck the ball, a man walked up behind me and without any hesitation began to shout, "Was that your ball? Did you look at it? That wasn't your ball; that was my ball! What kind of ball were you hitting?" The barrage of questions continued. I was shocked into disbelief. I was not even aware that the threesome in which he was playing was that close behind us. I was somewhat nonplussed by his attitude as I had never seen that kind of behavior on a golf course before (maybe I don't play enough golf), and then I felt remiss that I had not checked to see if that was my ball. I really did not know what to say. I apologized and began to walk away. My partner, observing this exchange, drove up in the cart and asked me where I had hit the ball. Fortunately, it was in the rough to the right of the green and not in the wild blue yonder where I often hit balls. He retrieved the ball, gave it to the man with an invitation to play through. The man accepted and we gladly let them play through.

When sharing this story with a friend of mine, he said, "All of that for a two-dollar ball." But life is like that. We can find ourselves irritated and even upset by the person in front of us in the grocery store check-out line who has twelve items in his basket in the "10-items-or-less" line. Road rage happens when drivers allow the poor driving behaviors of other drivers to determine their hand gestures, words shouted through a car window, or even how they drive their cars. Perspective is lost and one becomes incapable of managing one's own behavior.

Gaining perspective is not easy, but it is essential. As Heifetz and Linsky write, "Few practical ideas are more obvious or more critical than the need to get perspective in the midst of action."[2] Perspective comes from seeing more than the immediate present both in space and time. It calls for being in the game while at the same time recognizing that the game is bigger than we are and will last longer than the present moment. It is having an awareness of our own presence in a given setting while at the same time being able to stand back from that setting to see everything else that is going on, including our participation in it as well as the process of interaction. Heifetz and Linsky call this skill "getting off the dance floor and going to the balcony."[3]

This psychological distancing, if only briefly, provides people the opportunity to be better managers of their own behavior. It gives the rational and logical part of the brain time to overrule any knee-jerk reactions and gives greater capacity for creative and objective thinking. It gives time for God to be God in the process and not be excluded by anxious, out-of-control behavior. Distancing allows time to look through the eyes and mind of Christ at the one with whom we have the conflict.

In so looking, we will see another person who needs Christ and is loved as much by Christ as we are. It can make the difference between "stimulus-reaction" (the other person's words and our un-thought-out reaction) and "stimulus-response" (the other person's words and our thoughtful, reflective, non-reactive, response). A moment's pause may make the difference between a successful reconciliation process and a division that only grows wider and deeper.

Since each exchange of words in a conversation may lead to new thoughts and feelings, it is important that the process of going to the balcony be reiterative, not static, and therefore repeated many times during the exchange process. It is also important to see one's self as well as the other person in the process. This calls for setting aside those thoughts or plans of what we will say next while we are not truly listening to the other person. It calls for awareness of our words, voice tone and body language. It calls for being truly present with the other person while simultaneously seeing what others would see if they were looking down from the balcony with us.

Going to the balcony is an effort to make an objective observation of who we are and what we are saying about what we believe and value. If our behavior is out of line with our core values, beliefs and principles, we should stop, take a breath, and move to bring it back into alignment. This is a piece of taking the log out of our own eye during the time we are seeking to remove the speck from another's eye. It is finding that three-legged stool and sitting resoundedly on it. Though difficult, going to the balcony takes intentional thought and practice. However, being difficult does not deny its benefit to the God-directed process of reconciliation.

Some recorded events in the life of Jesus in the New Testament reflect this perspective. In the three years of his recorded public ministry, people were always trying to define Jesus' life for him. It began with his attending a wedding with his mother and disciples. When the supply of wine was almost diminished, his mother Mary turned to her son and mentioned this fact. There must have been some motherly imperative in this statement since his response was "Dear woman, why do you involve me; My time has not yet come"(Jn. 2:4).

In this apparently offensive situation of being low on wine, Jesus saw eternal implications. This was not just about him then, but about him the next day and forever. There was a bigger picture than was imminently evident. By his going to the balcony, he was able to put the current events into perspective and disallow the anxiety of the immediate circumstances to define his behavior. He was able to manage himself and chose a response that flowed from understanding the big picture, not just the pressing desires of an anxious wedding host.

Jesus maintained this sense of ultimate-cause-driven presence throughout his earthly life all the way through the crucifixion, burial, resurrection and ascension. There were many who tried to derail him over the course of his era-changing life, including the devil and some of Jesus' closest and uniquely chosen disciples, but he did not waiver. His knowing who he was and who sent him, while understanding the big picture of his mission and purpose, enabled him to withstand the efforts of both people and diabolic forces to get him to abandon the mission. About everything was tried, but it all failed. Though we will never be as self-controlled and self-regulated as Jesus was, by God's grace and through his Spirit, we have capacities for this behavior, and utilizing them in a reconciliation process is of the utmost value.

5. Where does anger fit in?

In the Gospel of Matthew, Jesus states, "If your brother sins against you, go and show him his fault. If he listens, you have won your brother over"(Mt. 18:15). In his letter to the Ephesians, Paul writes, "In your anger do not sin: Do not let the sun go down while you are still angry, and do not give the devil a foothold" (Eph 4:26-27). Jesus addresses the issue of sin and outlines steps to handle that matter while Paul notes that a person may be in the emotional state of anger, but that anger in and of itself is not sin, though it may lead to it.

Anger is a secondary emotional reaction that has underlying fears, hurts, threats, frustrations or anxieties triggering it. It is part of the emotional dynamic that existed in God and in God's creation before the fall. It is not sinful to be angry, as some anger may serve a useful purpose, e.g., being angry over slavery in the United States helped bring about changes in the law to help prevent discrimination against people by color. On the other hand, anger can be destructive if the laws enacted to protect some only elicit more racial hatred and discrimination. So that the latter does not happen, Paul encourages a timely addressing of the anger so something sinful or sinister does not develop because of it.

God created us as emotional beings so we could feel and have relationships as living beings and not function as inanimate robots. We were created to be connected to others and have interpersonal relationships with them. We are fashioned for community, and without community we could not be the body of Christ with all of its various parts (1 Cor.12:14-20).

Except for the three pastoral epistles (1-2 Timothy and Titus), all other epistles in the New Testament were written to communities of believers. In Luke's account of the early church after Pentecost and the coming of the Holy Spirit, he continually refers to "they" who were engaged in teaching, fellowship, breaking of bread and prayers and growing in numbers daily (Acts 2:42-47). In the eyes of God, the church is "where two or three are gathered in my name, there am I among them"(Mt. 18: 20 ESV). Therefore, no individual in the church can see himself as a unit unto himself and not a part of the community of interconnected believers and followers of Christ. Though it may manifest itself as a structural or organizational relationship, the church is an organic system of emotional, physical, rational and spiritual relationships. It has life and gives life. Though very complex, it is this abundance of gifts that gives connection to the non-churched world.

However, this system of relationships still exists on this side of heaven, and as Martin Luther noted, there are three forces of life that militate against the system working well, namely, the devil, the world and our sinful nature.

Consequently, all aspects of the organic system are subject to misuse and abuse.

As anxiety gets higher in one person, it spreads to other people in the organism. As anxiety increases, it is common for the emotional system to have dominance over a person's faith. As a result, the person's core values are set aside and clear thinking wanes. Instead of being faith-based communities with healthy relationships, churches and families become fractured and divided. The asset of having the capacity for relationship and being in community now serves counterproductive purposes.

In summary, with the capacity for community, relationships with others can be wholesome and life-giving. At the same time, the converse may be true. The capacity for community may lead some to be insensitive, haughty, rude, vicious, insolent and toxic toward others. The key is not to let the anger turn to sin, but to let the anger guide and direct to constructive, fruitful behavior.

6. Looking at the big picture

As emotional human beings with many different gifts, assets, strengths and virtues, as well as funny quirks, idiosyncrasies, unique mannerisms, habits and values, we may say and do things that elicit negative reactivity in others. It is not a matter of if, but when. It is simply impossible for all people to live in harmony with all other people all the time. We are too uniquely individualistic for that to be the case. The large number of stories in grocery store tabloids of marriages "made in heaven" breaking up within a few years, if not a few months, demonstrates the case.

Behavior by one person is not automatically evil or sin just because it is seen as such by another. It may lead to sin, but, in and of itself, may not be. Perhaps this understanding is what led the writer of Proverbs to state, "A man's wisdom gives him patience; it is to his glory to overlook an offense" (Pr. 19:11). Shortly thereafter he wrote, "It is to a man's honor to avoid strife, but every fool is quick to quarrel" (Pr. 20:3). Some matters in life, even disagreements or differences of opinion between people, are not sinful.

An emotional reaction may be beneficial to the one expressing it if it is owned by the one expressing it and not destructive to self or others. The non-destructive release of emotional energy may be healthier than denying or repressing it. The latter may lead to destruction of self (ramming a fist through a wall and breaking a wrist) or others (tongue lashing someone for a frivolous mistake). Therefore, as an act of care and concern for a person who engages in the reconciliation process *without* first 1) developing the healthy attitude of humility, 2) working on having a transformed heart and mind, and 3) growing in love and obedience, it is of value and wisdom to listen to that person's expressed emotions without taking it personally and without reacting to it as a personal attack.

Indeed, it is helpful to see the expressing of emotion as one person responding or reacting in a given way to a particular situation. What is said or done is that person's responsibility. We do not have to take responsibility for it or be defined by it. This calls for having some emotional boundaries that disallow the behavior of the other person to influence who we are and what we do. This is having a sense of self that is guided by an *internal* compass of faith, core values, beliefs and principles, and not *external* events, people or circumstances. Understanding these dynamics is not necessarily easy, nor will we ever be perfect at it, but spiritual and emotional maturity helps enable it to happen.

Reflections on Chapter 4

1. Of the hindrances to starting the reconciliation process, which one (s) would most describe why you would not enter into a reconciliation process? _____
_____
_____

2. Give a reason why a Christian should enter into a process of reconciliation even when there may be some <u>felt</u> reasons for not doing so. _____
_____
_____

3. What is the benefit of knowing "whose you are" before entering into a reconciliation process? _____
_____
_____

4. What does it mean to take the log out of your own eye before trying to remove the speck out of another person's eye? _____
_____

The Process of Reconciliation

5. In the reconciliation process you are encouraged to "put God first." What does that mean and how does one do it? ___

_____

_____

6. Anxiety, chronic and acute, reduces perspective. Objectivity and rational thinking take a back seat to reactivity and subjective thinking. The nose of the devil protrudes under the tent and seeks to get his whole body in. How does one gain or regain perspective when this happens? _____

_____

_____

7. Since most conflict involves some anger, how is the anger handled if reconciliation is to happen? _____

_____

_____

_____

Chapter 5

Understanding Values

Finally, beloved, whatever is true, whatever is honorable, whatever is just, whatever is pure, whatever is pleasing, whatever is commendable, if there is any excellence and if there is anything worthy of praise, think about these things. Keep on doing the things that you have learned and received and heard and seen in me, and the God of peace will be with you. Phil. 4:8, 9

In the previous chapters, there have been references to "values" in the shaping of our personalities and behaviors. In his book, *Peace in the Parish*, James Qualben identifies four levels of values and places them in quantifiable categories to help clarify how behavior based on a given value, as compared to another, may affect the outcome of a relationship or decision. Qualben identifies four values and the behaviors that reflect each. A working understanding of these levels is useful in discerning the basis for a conflict and some potential behaviors that would be helpful in working through it. It helps the creative, imaginative and executive part of the brain override the emotional part of the brain and therefore move a conflict onto a more harmonious playing field. In other words, it enables us to think before we act.

We function with many different values in life and all are needed to give it meaning. Values serve a variety of purposes. They help determine our thoughts and behavior as well as helping us assess the importance another person places on a given event or situation. For purposes of this book, values will be described as though they are entities on four floors of a building with a connecting link or elevator between the floors. Each value is basically confined to its own floor, but certain circumstances cause them to comingle. When this happens, conflict often happens. Therefore, understanding this value system can help in the reconciliation process when conflict arises. No value is better than another, but understanding their unique characteristics can help sort through the issues of life and discover where one should or should not put energy, time, thought and behavior.

A working definition of a value is the social principles, goals or standards held or accepted by an individual, class, society, etc. A value touches the heart and elicits strong emotions; it arouses action. Our values help define behavior, opinion, perceptions, and attitudes. They govern how we make decisions. Though not always acknowledged or understood, their ubiquitous presence prevents life without their influence. Therefore, what we value and what our values are make a difference.

A. Personal Preferences

Perhaps the easiest values to understand are what are called *personal-preference* (*first-level*) values. They help define us as individuals and are seen as the lowest or first level of values. These are kinetic and may change many times in a lifetime. They guide our preferences or choices about many decisions made on a daily basis, e.g., how we wear our hair, what clothes we put on each day, the brand and model of car we drive, our favorite sports team (if any), where we like to live, etc. Some are fluid and easily and quickly changed by external sources such as friends, advertising, shows on TV or the big screen, or other life experiences. They are identified by statements that begin with, "I like…" or "I don't like…"

For example, "I like Blue Bell gold rim homemade vanilla ice cream. I do not like Blue Bunny vanilla ice cream." "I like broccoli." "I hate broccoli."

Others personal-preference values may be deep rooted, based on some events in life that have embedded these thoughts in the mind. For example, my maternal grandfather said that he did not ever want to own a black car because the last car he would ride in would be black, and he did not want to ride in one before that day. This was at the turn of the twentieth century when most, if not all hearses, were black. Something about the color black associated with hearses led him to have this well-defined, personal-preference value. This value may or may not be shared by others, but it was his.

A personal-preference value is one into which all other values may collapse if tension or stress in the system gets high enough. For example, a church was building a new sanctuary and a fellowship hall that was to serve as a multi-purpose space. When it came to the floor covering for the fellowship hall, there was great debate over whether it should be a durable carpet or vinyl tile. This became no small issue and sides were taken, such that some threatened to leave the church if their position was not approved. Though there may have been discussion about doing what pleases God or picking the cheap or inexpensive one because that is better Christian stewardship, it became a personal-preference issue. What one liked or did not like in the form of floor covering for a fellowship hall became a defining value for many relationships. The argument became so heated that it threatened to divide the church.

In standing back from this issue, one could ask, how could this happen in a church where behavior is to be governed by the Gospel, love, grace and forgiveness? How could people fight and threaten to leave over something that no one will pay much attention to within weeks, if not days, after it is laid down. How could the anxiety in the system get so high over the floor covering in a fellowship hall that friendships turned sour and relationships were broken?

This is what happens when other values collapse into personal preference. It also may be the case that this behavior was, or became, sinful if it led to gossip, slander, name calling, blaming, threatening of withholding of funds if their choice of floor covering was not selected. If so, an intentional process of reconciliation should have begun among the people involved. If not, though the floor eventually got covered with something, this division could remain as a hindrance to the life and ministry of the congregation for years, if not decades. The same dynamic happens in families and businesses with the same result.

B. Institutional/Well-Being

The values with the next broader scope and those "higher" on the value scale are referred to as *institutional* or *well-being* values. These are considered *second-level* values. Values on this level govern decisions and the process for making decisions to maintain organization or structure. They help things work more smoothly and give a sense of order in the midst of chaos. They include state and federal laws, dress codes, liturgies, constitutions, formal and informal roles, rules, and regulations. Their governance is for the sake of maintaining uniformity, safety and a sense of like-mindedness. They engage the areas of power, authority, and control. They are less self-centered than the personal preference values and give an organization an endoskeleton upon which the various components relate and draw their meaning and purpose.

For example, in the church mentioned above, the method of addressing the conflict came through its constitution and by-laws, which prescribed the use of *Robert's Rules of Order* for conducting business. A proper meeting was called of those who could legally vote according to the constitution. Following *Robert's Rules of Order*, the congregation voted in the prescribed manner and a decision was made. Though the decision was not made for either carpeting or for vinyl tile but to cover one-half the floor with carpeting and one-half with vinyl tile, a decision was made, and it was made utilizing second-level values. Though first-level values were still very operative, the actual decision-making process followed a prescribed way of making group decisions as outlined in the congregationally approved constitution. Had there not been operative second-level values, there may have been a split in the church with either the carpet people or the vinyl tile people leaving. One group would have left to start the church of the carpeted floors or the church of the vinyl floors, and left the other group to do the opposite.

C. Identity

The next tier up in the value scale is referred to as *identity* values. These *third-level* values name and locate us within the larger scheme of things. On this level, the early church followers of Jesus Christ as Lord and Savior were called "Christian" (Acts 11:26; 26:28; 1 Pt. 4:16) or "the Way"

(Acts 18:25, 26; 19:9, 23) to give them their own identity and to distinguish them from being a Jewish sect. Though the distinguishing characteristics are being blurred by taking a variety of positions on various issues, many Christians in America still differentiate themselves from one another by denominational identity, e.g., Methodist, Baptist, Catholic, Lutheran, Presbyterian, and Episcopalian. There are other groupings, e.g., Evangelical, Pentecostal, and Charismatic. Others call themselves interdenominational or non denominational. All give some sense of identity that connects the organization and its organizational structure values (second level) to its reason and purpose for existence (fourth level).

In the secular world, the right to strike is an identity-level value for organized labor, which itself is an organization based on an identity-level value. Various community, social and political organizations give one a sense of belonging and a unique identity as being this and not that. License plate frames claiming membership in an alumni association from a particular university as well as the insignia on the back of a shirt or jacket while riding in a pod of motorcycles give one a sense of belonging and connectivity. There is a sense of being or belonging to one group or organization while not being or belonging to another. A sense of identity is created that helps draw boundaries. Some people are in and some are not.

While third-level values give one a sense of being a part of a whole that is greater than the sum of its parts, the organization is still made up of individuals. As an organization, it will have agreed that there will be certain rules, guidelines, policies or procedures for conducting the "business" of the organization (second level). However, as noted when discussing second-level values, first-level values may still become operative in the life of the organization. For example, if one person during a church meeting states, "I don't care what the policy is, or what Scripture says, I don't like it, and I'm not going to approve sending any more money to missions," the organization is potentially drawn into first-level thinking. To the speaker, personal preference is more important than any policy (second level), corporate identity (third level), or ultimate purpose for the policy, even if it is from Scripture (fourth level).

However, what happens next will determine if the conversation stays there. If a response to this statement by another participant in the meeting is "That's stupid. I can't imagine you acting so childish," first-level values will remain operative, and more aggressive verbal behavior may come forth until it is stopped. If, on the other hand, one who is thoughtful and not fused into reactivity behavior addresses it in a calm voice, the issues and interests of the original speaker may be addressed without creating more division. Someone who, intuitively or otherwise, understands a hierarchical value system may also address it. The person calmly seeks the floor from the chairperson and suggests that now would be a good time to take a break and perhaps say a prayer for God to provide wisdom and understanding. In so doing, the focus of the meeting is changed and higher-level values are brought to bear upon the situation.

Third-level values are bridge values. They create a link between second-level values, which create and provide a sense of order and structural purpose, with *fourth-level* values that are the *lordship* or *ultimate-purpose* values. Third-level values can be used as a facade or mask to conceal or masquerade first-level or second-level thinking. For example, while a person may be using third-level words like Christian, Lutheran, Diocese, Presbytery, Synod, American or Canadian, that person may be really espousing a personal position based on a first-level meaning of that word. When this happens at a congregational, regional or national level of an organization, conflict usually develops and is fought at second-level values where the formality of making motions, seconding motions and voting provides a venue for the conflict to be officially waged.

Litigation also may be introduced as a second-level mode of addressing differences. If there is little capacity within the organization to gain and retain behavior motivated by fourth-level values, at the most, second-level values will dominate. What happens at third-level values must always be connected to fourth-level values or behavior will collapse *formally* into second-level values and *informally* into first-level values. The anxiety in the system will lead to this collapse.

The Pharisees in the New Testament modeled this reality. They had an identity in the larger church as being Pharisees (third level), and they championed the laws of God and being obedient to him as their Lord (fourth level). However, their behavior hardly broke the surface of being above second-level values. For example, in the book of Matthew we read, "But when the Pharisees saw this (Jesus' disciples picking and eating grain on the Sabbath because they were hungry), they said to Him, 'Look, your disciples do what is not lawful to do on a Sabbath'" (Mt. 12:2 NRSV).

In an apparent effort to reflect their commitment to God and be faithful to him (fourth level), the Pharisees accused Jesus' disciples of doing what they themselves say they would not have done, i.e., publicly break one of the laws that God himself had given (second level). They wanted to focus on the disciples' disobedience and, in so doing, discredit Jesus. On both an organizational (second level) and a personal (first level) level they saw him as a threat ("*Your disciples...*"). By speaking as Pharisees (third level), i.e., having a position of high standing in the church, their statements would have apparent credulity to those who heard this chastisement of Jesus.

Inasmuch as he was attacked at first and second levels, Jesus' response to this assault was not to attack the Pharisees personally (first level) nor discuss with them their emphasis on a legalistic, narrowly-defined interpretation of the law (second level) but to shed light on the true meaning, purpose and will of God (fourth level) when he said:

> Haven't you read what David did when he and his companions were hungry? He entered the house of God, and he and his companions ate the consecrated bread—which was not lawful for them to do, but only for the priests. Or haven't you read in the Law that on the Sabbath the priests in the temple desecrate the day and yet are innocent? I tell you that one

greater than the temple is here. If you had known what these words mean, 'I desire mercy, not sacrifice,' you would not have condemned the innocent (Mt. 12:3-7).

Jesus did not regress to their level of functioning but brought to bear the true meaning and value of the law and his place as the Redeemer in it. Just as was noted earlier when discussing the *going-to-the-balcony* concept, Jesus again was able to stand back from the foray of the moment and not allow it to define him, but for him to define it.

Shortly thereafter, Jesus went into the synagogue and healed the shriveled hand of a male worshiper. Upon observing this miracle of Jesus, the Pharisees began looking for reasons to accuse Jesus of breaking other laws. In spite of what they had just previously heard from Jesus, they were focused on, and fused into, maintaining their interpretation of the law (second level). Since having and maintaining laws are beneficial to organizations and countries, having them, in and of itself, is not an issue. The issue here, and as it becomes in many organizations (congregations included), is that once established, the maintenance of them moves from being a servant of the identity (third level) and lordship values (fourth level) to being the sole purpose for the existence of the organization.

Later, in this same text, it is noted that the Pharisees "went out and plotted how they might kill Jesus"(Mt. 12:14). Their apparent indignation over Jesus' intentional violation of the laws, as they understood them, led them to lose any sense of objectivity or discernment of who God was and what the purpose of the laws were, i.e., to maintain a healthy relationship with the living and creating God by trusting him and being obedient to him. Instead, their emotions overrode their ability to be rational, and they became focused on killing Jesus. They could not see any other choice. The emotional process was activated, and they were blinded by passion, both individually and collectively. As individuals and as a group, the behavior of the Pharisees had regressed to first-level thinking, and not only as an emotion but, in fact, as a violation of the law, "You shall not murder" (Ex. 20:13 ESV). The paradox, and they did not seem to see it, was that they were willing to violate one law while condemning Jesus to death for healing a disabled man on the Sabbath. They were willing to kill because he gave life. Again, the anxiety in the system disallowed them from going to the balcony and getting off the dance floor.

Though the proposed actions that the Pharisees plotted at that time are not usually seen in the church today, at least in America or Canada, the depth of reactivity that the Pharisees reflected is. It may not be as blatant and transparent, but it is present nonetheless. It may manifest itself in more "civil" forms like parking lot meetings, phone calls, letter writing, voice-mail messages, hostile e-mail, text messages, Twitter postings, blogs, web pages and cliques or reactionary groups.

Reactivity may show up in subtle efforts to sabotage the integrity and veracity of another through gossip, rumor, blame, and innuendo. It may take place by planting seeds of doubt or discontent in the minds of others while showing a face of cooperativeness and support. Those who participate in such activities, not unlike the Pharisees, do so with the thought that what they are doing is important and necessary for maintaining or saving the church. The perceived purpose, in their mind, is good, but the motives behind the behavior may be sinful and even diabolical.

D. Lordship/Ultimate Purpose

The fourth and final level of values is, as has been referred to many times, the *lordship* or *ultimate* values. These values reflect what gives the vital meaning and significance to life.

They are preeminent over all other values and lead to the ultimate definitions and understandings of life. They govern our functioning and lead to behavior based on principles and ethics understood as being revelatory from the ultimate source of life. As Christians, this life source is God in three persons, Father, Son and Holy Spirit, as succinctly summarized in the Apostles' Creed. He and all that is to be known about him are revealed in Scripture and are opened to us through the power of the Holy Spirit.

Though ultimate values may not regulate or determine the color of the shirt we wear to the office on Tuesday or whether we eat a hamburger or a steak for dinner on Thursday, they play a part in the decision. For example, there may be a dress code for our office (second level). Wearing a particular type of clothing may be in violation of this code. We may disagree with this code and begin to think about how we will respond. First-level thinking may lead us to think to ourselves or say to others, "The code is stupid; I will wear what I want to," and do so.

Second-level thinking may lead us along the same process, but we choose to obey the code because it is the code or we use a prescribed process for dissent and bring the concerns to management. Third-level thinking may lead us to having the same concern but recognizing that the organization would like to present a given image to the public, and the dress code reflects that corporate identity. We wear the prescribed clothing because we subscribe to that identity.

Fourth-level thinking, again, may lead our thoughts in the same direction, but we wear the prescribed clothing because doing so reflects our integrity and desire to do what is for the common good of the whole company. For Christians, this fourth-level response may flow out of the summary of our obedience to God: "'Love the Lord your God with all your heart and with all your soul and with all your strength and with all your mind'; and, 'Love your neighbor as yourself'" (Luke 10:27). For non-Christians, other statements that define essential reasons for existence and purpose of life may be operative.

What is important to us, and how we allow that importance to regulate behavior, does make a difference in the life and ministry of the body of Christ. For some people fourth-level values, though articulated verbally, have little or no impact on daily behavior. Parishioners may worship regularly with other believers, express a belief and trust in Jesus as their Lord and Savior, pray the Lord's Prayer, and say from memory the Apostles' Creed but live lives that show little resemblance to this expressed and confessed faith.

Their lives in the *real* world are significantly different than their lives in the presence of others in the worshiping community. Because of our sinful nature, this is true of all Christians some of the time, but for some people it is true most of the time. It is this behavior that leads others, especially non-Christians, to see the Christian church as hypocritical. Jesus said it this way: "These people honor me with their lips, but their hearts are far from me. They worship me in vain; their teachings are but rules taught by men" (Mt. 15:8-9).

However, many Christians live out fourth-level values as a way of life. These are core values to them and are manifested, publicly or privately, in their daily behavior. Their hearts and minds are being transformed and reshaped by the work of the Holy Spirit. Paul grasped the reality of this process as he wrote to the Roman Christians:

> Therefore, since we have been justified through faith, we have peace with God through our Lord Jesus Christ, through whom we have gained access by faith into this grace in which we now stand. And we rejoice in the hope of the glory of God. Not only so, but we also rejoice in our sufferings, because we

know that suffering produces perseverance; perseverance, character; and character, hope. And hope does not disappoint us, because God has poured out his love into our hearts by the Holy Spirit, whom he has given us (Rom. 5:1-5).

Reflections on Chapter 5

1. Give examples of some of your personal-preference values. _____
_____
_____

2. How have these values affected your relationship with others? _____
_____
_____

3. What is the benefit of having institutional-level values in an organization? _____
_____
_____

4. What identity-level values are operative in your life?
_____
_____

5. How can identity-level values really be personal-preference values in disguise? _____
_____
_____

6. How easy is it to keep lordship values operative in times of conflict? _____
How can they become operative? _____
_____

Chapter 6

Getting to the Heart of the Matter (Taking Action)

Brothers, if someone is caught in a sin, you who are spiritual should restore him gently. But watch yourself, or you also may be tempted. Carry each other's burdens, and in this way you will fulfill the law of Christ. If anyone thinks he is something when he is nothing, he deceives himself. Each one should test his own actions. Then he can take pride in himself, without comparing himself to somebody else, for each one should carry his own load. Gal. 6:1-5

Therefore, as God's chosen people, holy and dearly loved, clothe yourselves with compassion, kindness, humility, gentleness and patience. Bear with each other and forgive whatever grievances you may have against one another. Forgive as the Lord forgave you. And over all these virtues put on love, which binds them all together in perfect unity. Col. 3:12-14

Is any one of you in trouble? He should pray. Is anyone happy? Let him sing songs of praise. Is any one of you sick? He should call the elders of the church to pray over him and anoint him with oil in the name of the Lord. And the prayer offered in faith will make the sick person well; the Lord will raise him up. If he has sinned, he will be forgiven. Therefore confess your sins to each other and pray for each other so that you may be healed. The prayer of a righteous man is powerful and effective. Ja. 5:13-16

Elijah was a man just like us. He prayed earnestly that it would not rain, and it did not rain on the land for three and a half years. Again he prayed, and the heavens gave rain, and the earth produced its crops.

My brothers, if one of you should wander from the truth and someone should bring him back, remember this: Whoever turns a sinner from the error of his way will save him from death and cover over a multitude of sins. Ja. 5:17-20

While it is important to understand family systems, values systems, hindrances to reconciliation process and core values indigenous in individuals involved in conflict resolution, it is ultimately essential that action be taken. Having all the right ingredients to bake a cake does not make a cake. Likewise in the reconciliation process, action needs to happen and energy needs to be expended. All the ingredients need to be present and brought together though there is neither prescribed quantities nor a prescribed time. The goal is reconciliation, and there cannot be too much of what helps the process work.

In starting the process and building on the three-legged stool of 1) having a Christ-like humble attitude, 2) having a transformed heart and mind, and 3) growing in obedience and love, it is important to identify process components significant in bringing about in-depth, heart-felt reconciliation.

A. Pray

Before, during and after an encountering of another person for the sake of reconciliation, one should be involved in prayer. As recorded in the Gospel of Matthew, Jesus tells us: "You have heard that it was said, 'Love your neighbor and hate your enemy.' But I tell you: Love your enemies and pray for those who persecute you, that you may be sons of your Father in heaven" (Mt. 5:43-45). James, the brother of Jesus, also encourages us to pray for each other: "Therefore, confess your sins to each other and pray for each other so that you may be healed. The prayer of a righteous man is powerful and effective" (Ja. 5:16-17). Since reconciliation, as it is being addressed here, is as much about God as it is about humanity, then God should be the first part, and prayer puts the matter front and center in the eyes of God.

The prayers should include the request for wisdom and understanding, for a peaceful and productive process, for God's will to be done, for healing, for forgiveness, for a change of heart for self and the other, for new life and new hope and for continued healthy dialog if the first step does not produce a God-pleasing outcome. The engaging of God through prayer in the process allows us to recognize and acknowledge God's movement toward us and his gift of grace. It puts aside our desires, sinful or otherwise, and lets the serendipitous nature of the Holy Spirit move in the process. It allows for an outcome that neither party would have anticipated before the process began. We need to seek and to knock in good faith, and he will bring insights, thoughts, words and outcomes not conceived without his presence. "Commit to the LORD whatever you do, and your plans will succeed" (Prov.16:3).

Prayer helps us go to the balcony and see ourselves, as well as others, as a part of what is going on. It brings God into the conciliation process and helps move the dialog from a potential first-level "he said, she said" to an upper-level discussion of the underlying interests and issues that are more foundational to the crisis than the presenting problems that became the focal point of the disagreement. This matter needs to be brought into the arena of the divine so the outcome flows through the divine into the broken. Just as God came to us through the incarnation of Christ in Jesus, he comes to us through the Holy Spirit in matters of reconciliation. There is a real presence of God. The playing field or stage is being redefined. The matter is no longer just a matter between two or more people, but a matter between two or more people and God, and that makes all the difference.

B. Mental Preparedness

Reread the Bible passages at the beginning of this section. All have words of wisdom in preparation for entering into the formal reconciliation process. They encourage addressing a brother or sister who has erred for his or her sake. Test your motives to make sure they are pure. Be ready and willing to acknowledge what you have contributed to the issue. Conflict never happens in a vacuum and is not singularly caused. It happens in a system that is always redefining itself, and causation is not always discernable, so do not become stuck on "the problem." Looking for someone or something to blame is not as beneficial as looking for a healthy outcome. Keep a focus on the process and the potential benefit that can come out of the discussion.

In an effort to find quiet and solitude from the crowds in Capernaum who were following him because of his teaching and performing of miracles, Jesus instructed his disciples to launch a boat to cross to the other side of the Sea of Galilee.

They did as he had directed. "Without warning, a furious storm came up on the lake, so that the waves swept over the boat. However, Jesus was sleeping. The disciples went and woke him saying, 'Lord, save us! We're going to drown!'" (Mt. 8:23-25). The disciples were certain that they would drown immediately. They saw no possible solution to an apparently imminent watery demise. It seems as if they really did not know what Jesus could or would do.

In grasping for a solution, any solution, the disciples focused their attention on the one who seemed to be doing the least to address the crisis at hand. In essence, they were saying, "*You* do something! We (experienced fishermen) have done all we can and it is not working. After all, you said 'follow me.' We did, and now we're going to die!" Jesus, in his ability not to get caught up in their anxiety, calmly said, "'You of little faith, why are you so afraid?' He then got up and rebuked the winds and the waves, and it was completely calm" (Mt. 8:26).

While the disciples focused on the problem and the apparent absence of potential solutions, they sought to place the responsibility somewhere else, not unlike what we do. Instead of getting caught up in their thinking, which had led them to see no solution, Jesus saw possibilities they had not considered. It is this type of thinking that is essential in the reconciliation process. Granted, we may not be able to calm a storm with a single spoken word, but by maintaining a healthy sense of being that is not caught up in emotional reactivity of the situation (regardless of how much the other people may want us to), we may help lead to outcomes inconceivable if this position had not been taken. Maintaining a healthy sense of self will bring calmness to the discussion and increases the potential of a mutually acceptable outcome.

In the story of the prodigal son, the son mentally prepared himself for the encounter with his father by thoughtfully reflecting on his present condition, developing a humble attitude, then rehearsing in his mind the exact words he would say to his father when he met him. He started with his own brokenness and contrite heart and acknowledged his sin before God and his father. He did not demand of his father that he forgive him or accept him back as son, but humbly confessed his sin and unworthiness to be his son. His mental preparation took time, which gave him opportunity to formulate a succinct, well-thought-out, non-reactive, non-judgmental, non-criticizing statement of contrition. He did not seek to blame his father or brother for the state of his life. He did not demand reacceptance, nor did he ask for more money so he could continue his out-of-control lifestyle. His mental preparation helped him be calm, which helped reduce the potential tension in the engagement with his father.

We see similar thinking by Jacob in his potentially volatile confrontation with his brother, Esau, as recorded in Genesis 33. From birth, Jacob was a thorn in the flesh of his brother. As the twins were born, Esau came out first from their mother's womb, but his younger brother was clutching his heel (Gen. 25:26). Consequently, he was named Jacob, i.e., he supplants. Later, when their aging father, Isaac, was to pass on the blessing to Esau, Jacob, with the help of his mother, stole the birthright. That which was to go to Esau came to Jacob, and it could not be reversed.

In time the brothers parted ways and each became wealthy in his own right. After many years of living in the "east" and serving as a very successful shepherd for Laban, the father of his two wives, Rachel and Leah, Jacob heard a calling from the Lord to return to his homeland. While on his journey home with his family and all his possessions, he encountered Esau. Anticipating a hostile reception, Jacob developed a strategy as to how he could confront his brother without bringing back all the hatred from the past. Once the plan was devised, he put it into action.

Observing that Esau had 400 men with him, Jacob decided to disarm Esau's fury by sending women and children first to greet him. He and his favorite wife would be last. Either the strategy worked and/or other conciliatory factors came into play, as it is recorded in Genesis 33:4, "Esau ran to meet him, and embraced him, and fell on his neck and kissed him, and they wept." This is a description, word-for-word of the behavior of the prodigal son's father once he had seen his son returning home. The planning ahead in a mindset of humility significantly benefits the reconciliation process.

C. Build a Bridge

The mental preparedness as described above is the first component of building a bridge to the other party in the dispute. It sets the tone and content of the initial contact. It creates a venue for a God-pleasing purpose and positive, desired outcome. It turns down the volume control on the potential static that comes from being unprepared. It reduces being sidetracked, derailed or sabotaged by extraneous matters and keeps the main thing the main thing.

The third component, building a relational bridge, moves the action toward the other and is designed to enable open and thoughtful communication. It is the doing or behavioral component of the reconciliation process.

Building a bridge begins with making a contact with the other person. A good way to begin is to start with where you are and your hurts, not with the other person and what that person did. A principle of relationships is this: people are not listening to you until they are emotionally moving toward you. Consequently, if you begin the reconciliation process by calling the offender on the phone to attack or accuse, the chances of the process working are slim and none. Defenses will be raised, objectivity and openness will be diminished, and the matter of the original conflict will now be confounded with a new issue, your attack. The primary issue will be lost, and a new source of division will arise.

In an effort to have the other person move emotionally toward you, after making contact and discerning if it is a good time to talk, ask a few questions about the other person. These questions could focus on family or job. If you are aware of some significant issues in the other person's life, ask questions about those matters and be genuinely concerned. Really listen. Listen to words, emotions and tone. This is not a game. This is not a ploy to manipulate. This is seeking to bring healing where healing is needed.

After establishing a credible relationship, it would be helpful to give a brief statement of why you called. Explain that you are hurting over brokenness in this relationship and that you would like assistance in healing. Seek permission to continue. An example of some words that may be helpful is, "About three weeks ago while we were together at the school board meeting, you said '...' Perhaps I misunderstood what you said, but I found what I thought you said offensive. I regret it now, but I did not say anything to you then. Since then I have not been able to forget it and have become angry and resentful toward you. I do not like feeling this way and regret it deeply. I would like to clear things up. By this phone call, I am asking you to meet with me so I may address this matter with you. Could we talk about it now or would you be willing to meet with me soon so we could talk face to face? I would greatly appreciate the opportunity to meet with you."

This statement identifies the issue while also taking ownership or responsibility for one's own feelings. It also identifies a desired outcome while striving to present a neutral position, not blaming the other person. This is important to understand, as we often want to blame others for what *they* did or said and how it made *us* feel. Properly understood, the behavior that elicited the response was *theirs*; it was not ours; however, the response to that behavior was *ours* and *they did not cause* it. As much as we would like to lay the blame and responsibility of our behavior at the foot of others, it just is not possible. Making and understanding this distinction early in the process is crucial.

Our reaction or response to a given stimulus (words, behaviors, mannerisms of others) is *our* reaction or response to that stimulus. The same stimulus may not elicit the same response or reaction in another person. While we may get angry or upset at a given statement, someone else may dismiss it as meaningless. They really hear and respond to the statement differently. Not all emotional systems are wired the same, and the system keeps changing with each new input.

Therefore, to blame another person for how we react in a given situation is an effort to deny our responsibility for our own behavior while shifting focus onto the other person. It gives permission to the other person or the situation or circumstances to determine how our lives will be lived. It is a giving up of our "self" to become a "non-self."

Blaming another is a boundaries issue. It allows the behavior of another to determine what is important to us and how we will live our lives. Emotionally, we allow the other person's stuff to slop over into our lives, and we do not stop it. In essence, we are saying, "I can't stop you from affecting my behavior, and I will blame you for how I am reacting." This may sound strange, but the more we think this cannot happen to us, the more it can and will.

Therefore, in an effort to bring a vulnerable, healthy self to the process, start with a question that invites the other person into a process to discuss our reaction to something that was said or done. In most cases, people will agree to participate in the process. This is not a bait and switch technique. This is not an effort to get someone to agree to walk with us through this process and then launch an attack once we have gotten that person to participate. With honesty and integrity we want to address the issues that affect the relationship by bringing them into the light and thereby putting them onto a stage of healthy discussion and interchange.

D. Managing the Process

Before meeting with the other person, prepare yourself by rereading the guidelines for mental and spiritual preparation for this time. Understand the value-system concepts so you have the capacity to move among the values and not become stuck on first-level values. Understand your interests. Have mental clarity as to why this encounter is taking place and what some desired outcomes might be. Intentionally seek to "remove the log from your own eye," and keep in mind the "going to the balcony" principle.

The meeting place, if the matter is not handled on the phone, should be a neutral space acceptable to both parties. If possible, sit in comfortable chairs at a comfortable social distance with no table or other object between the two of you. Good lighting and ventilation are desired. Be on time. Allow significant time in your schedule, and do not try to rush the process.

Begin with a greeting and a "thank you" to the other person for coming and participating in the process. Create a congenial relationship by asking questions of the other person. If this is a face-to-face meeting after the initial phone contact, again ask questions about any important issues that may be significant in that person's life at that time. Maintain good eye contact and focus on the other person, the intended objective of the meeting, and being present. If you have a cell phone and bring it along, turn it off or turn it to vibrate. If your phone does vibrate, check to see who is calling. If it is not a crisis or an emergency, either do not answer it or answer it, and tell the other person that you are busy and will call them back. Stay the course of the purpose of the meeting, and do not become derailed by what may seem to be urgent, but not important.

The process of reconciliation will call for identifying the behavior of the other person that led to your own reaction. It is important that this not be soft peddled nor overly exaggerated. It needs to be addressed forthrightly, with integrity and without condemning or judging the other. Care enough about yourself, the other person, and the relationship between the two of you to confront the other person with a desire to understand the other's interests and bring clarity and healing to the broken relationship

In his book, *Caring Enough to Confront*, David Augsburger identifies this behavior as "care-fronting."[4] While genuinely caring for the other, the behavior of the other is confronted. This concept cannot be stated more succinctly and clearly than in the words of Paul: "But speaking the truth in love, we must grow up in every way into him who is the head, into Christ, from whom the whole body, joined and knit together by every ligament with which it is equipped, as each part is working properly, promotes the body's growth in building itself up in love" (Eph. 4:15-16 NRSV).

"Care-fronting" expresses concern for relationship and the health of the body of Christ while promoting growth by challenging behavior that is destructive to the body. Out of concern for body health, one member of the body reflects enough maturity and assertiveness to address another member of the body in a way that will be perceived as both loving and challenging. The effort is not to sugarcoat the issue, but to present it in a way that brings the behavior out of darkness into the light while not destroying the other person. If the behavior is sinful, the sin cannot be denied. At the same time, if the sin is acknowledged with a contrite heart and confessed, absolution cannot be denied either.

As a tool to help manage the process:

a. On a 3 X 5 card briefly write about the specific incident, issue, or hurt that has broken the relationship and needs to be addressed. See diagrams below for structure and content to include on the each card. Use one card for each incident or hurt to be addressed.

Front

What happened—(What the conflict is about, i.e., the issue.) What was said or done that was the offense to me? (Be specific.)

My reaction to the issue—As I think about the event, what am I thinking and feeling? (Be specific.)

Back

> What I needed most from you in that situation—What would have been helpful for you to do or say, or not do or say?
>
> Briefly note a God-pleasing, healthy desired outcome. (This can help keep the conversation focused.)

b. For seven days pray over the cards. Seek God's guidance and leadership in your response to the other in a reconciliation process. Be intentional about separating the presenting **issue** ("what happened" on front of card), your **reaction** to the issue (your level of reactivity to the issue), your **needs** or **position** relative to that issue (what would have been helpful at that time/now), and your **interests** (what a God-pleasing, healthy outcome looks like). The interests are the motivators that underline a position and reflect our values, concerns, desires, needs or limitations. They may be concrete or abstract and give meaning and purpose to life.

c. After seven days assess where you are spiritually, emotionally and relationally with the other person. That matter may, by God's grace, already be reconciled. If so, overlook the matter as guided in Proverbs 12:16, "A fool shows his annoyance at once, but a prudent man overlooks an insult." If not, reevaluate your needs and position, as they may have changed, and continue with the care-fronting reconciliation process. The desire is to address the issue with the highest level of spiritually healthy care-fronting and the lowest level of attack, i.e., "setting things straight" or "fixing the other person."

d. After making arrangements to meet the other, take the cards and use them as resources to stay focused on the matters at hand. Do not attack the other person, but express yourself using the information on the card (s) as an outline. After reading or paraphrasing what is written on the card, ask the other to respond, then listen, LISTEN, LISTEN. Stay in control of yourself and do not get reactive to the other person's responses and create a whole new conflict.

There is a good chance that the other person may be guarded and defensive. As this process is uncomfortable for you, it is for the other person as well. It may be awkward and stilted at first, but with winsome tenacity it can be productive. If necessary, at the beginning make a light comment about being nervous about this process and therefore you wrote down some notes to keep you on track. A prayer at the beginning will set the stage for a healthy interchange.

Remember the five hindrances to the reconciliation process: a) not knowing what to say, b) thinking the other person will not listen, c) leaving it alone; it is not as bad as it seems d) fearing losing, and e) fearing that the other person always wins. The other person may be experiencing one or more of these and feel threatened by the process. Manage yourself and strive not to manage the other. This process takes time. It is not a timed game in which there is a winner and a loser.

e. If you are the one with which the other has conflict, listen. Listen to the words as the words are significant. However, there is more to the communication process than just words. Volume, tone of voice and body language are more powerful than words alone. Listen to all communication expressions, and, despite what may be your own initial response to the expression of an issue, seek to understand before being understood. Do not judge, criticize, dismiss, correct or blame.

If clarity is needed, ask questions for clarity, not questions to get data to validate what you said or why you said it. If needed, reframe or restate what you think you heard in order to gain clarity and understanding. The desire of the other person coming to you is to seek a reconciled relationship. Honor that decision. As it may have been difficult for you to come to that person, it may also have been difficult for that person to come to you. The process is more important than the content, and a healthy relationship is more important than winning. This is about life in the body of Christ, and the body loses if one member of it destroys another. For the sake of the whole, both need to be healthy.

f. As each person becomes more transparent and vulnerable to the other in a trusting relationship, e.g., Jacob to Esau and the prodigal son to his father, the process moves forward. The process reaches a moment of significance when one person asks the other to forgive his behavior (words, gestures, attacks, innuendo, etc.) that created offense and broke relationship. Based on God's forgiving us as we forgive others (the Lord's Prayer), the hearer of these words is compelled in obedience to his loving God to forgive. This is not an option but an automatic expression of love and mercy that flows from a transformed and renewed heart.

Inasmuch as forgiveness is a vital component of reconciliation, the process is as much an art as a science. It is as much an act of the heart as it is the head. It is as much an aspect of the will as it is of behavior. It is as much a course of change as it is a point in time. It is more fluid than solid and is more what happens than what one controls. Consequently, the process is not a set of lock-step procedures that once completed produces the desired outcome. It is a journey that should not be rushed, but it should be embraced with intentionality. It may be scary or difficult to begin, and we may trip and fall a number of times, but once on the path there is a potential for a newness of life that comes no other way.

E. Care-Listening

As noted above, listening to the other person, *really* listening to the other person, is a significant piece of the reconciliation process. In the arena of conflict, it is very difficult to listen to the other person. Our physical and emotional resources are gearing up for war, and our brain is working overtime to protect the system. Our brain can function much faster than the other person can speak. Therefore, while that person is speaking, at one level we are sensing tone of voice, body language, words and expressions. At another level we are creating our own reactive defense and justification for our behavior. Resourcefulness and objectivity are lost in the tyranny of the anxious moment. We are not listening neutrally, but listening through a filtering system that eliminates some, if not all, credibility or integrity in the other person.

Therefore, we need a listening manner that removes the filters and enables a neutral and open listening process.

Some components of this listening process are the following:

a. *Want* to care enough to listen to the other person. Since reconciliation is the desired outcome, be motivated by that outcome to do all you are consciously aware of to bring about that objective. Do not treat the process like a game or frivolous task, but be engaged in it.

b. Make a *commitment* to the care-listening task. Stick to the task of listening. This does not mean you never talk, but it does mean you have an understanding that if the other person never feels understood, then that person will not feel accepted, and if not accepted then reconciliation cannot take place. Psychological research has demonstrated that we all like to feel significant. Significance comes when we feel that not only are our words heard, but also our underlying interests and needs are understood. It is here that our hearts and souls are revealed.

c. Be *patient*. Not every silence has to be filled with words, especially ours. The author of Ecclesiastes writes there is "a time to be silent and a time to speak"(Eccl. 3:7b). Being silent and intentionally listening to another, which includes not only words but also tonal inflection and body language, is one of the most difficult behaviors to undertake. In our hurry-up, fast-paced world, we want and expect immediate responses. Conversations with long pauses, even as short as one or two seconds, become irritants, especially for those who are "action" oriented vis-à-vis those who are more "thought" oriented. Many believe silence is negative and therefore to be avoided even if *the listener* has to fill the void. In so doing, the original speaker is denied his chance to speak, and the listener is denied his opportunity to listen and learn.

d. Know one's own *boundaries*. Do not become a rescuer. Some people like to be "fixers" or "rescuers." They have a propensity to be problem solvers. If there is a need, they want to fill it. If there is a problem, they want to solve it. If there is something broken, they want to fix it. They may not be aware of it, but there is a sense of willfulness about their behavior. They often have the solution to a problem before they ever fully hear or understand it. They stop listening when they think they have heard enough information for them to discern a solution. It may not be a good or the right solution, but in their minds, it is both. Consequently, these people can easily impose their thinking or values on others and not realize they are doing it. They are just doing what comes naturally. Therefore, they may try to bring closure or conclusion to a matter that in the minds of the other is still very open. While they are saying "What's the big deal, get over it" or "Well, that settles that," the other party still feels unheard. The reconciliation process calls for the listener to have some boundaries on his desire to quickly rescue. Slow down and let the process work.

On the other hand, those who like to think things through need to realize that not all people are like them either. There are those who are wired for action, and processing matters over time is painful. It seems to be a waste of time. Therefore, if your conflict is with a more action-oriented person than you are, realize, acknowledge and honor that person's needs as well. Strive to stay connected, and address issues in a succinct manner without a lot of fluff. Do not be abrasive or offensive, but care enough to strive to work on the offense in a way that acknowledges the other's needs as well as your own.

One way to determine if good listening is taking place and the process is leading to closure or reconciliation is the presence or absence of the words "Yes, but..." or other words that indicate the speaker feels unheard or not fully heard. If you think you have been a good listener and you sense healthy closure is taking place and you start moving in that direction and the other person says, "Yes, but…," this is a red flag indicating that the matter has not yet been fully addressed. It would be helpful to explore this concern and, in so doing, determine if it fits into the purpose of this discussion. If it does fit, address it. If it does not fit, set it aside to be addressed later. Remember, the desired outcome is reconciliation, not the quick fix, and practicing good listening skills is a key ingredient to the process. Conflicts, like physical wounds that prematurely heal only from the outside, are apt to fester and erupt at a future time. Therefore, be prepared to meet a number of times to address the issues properly and fully.

Realize also that some issues may not be resolved to the desired outcome of either person. Every family and every relationship has some irreconcilable differences. If it is at all possible, for the sake of the relationship and one's own health, heed the wisdom of Christ when he warns us about swallowing camels while trying to strain out gnats (Mt. 23:24). In an effort to get every "i" dotted and every "t" crossed, we may over focus on what is wrong and broken and not on what is right or where there is agreement. This calls for a trip to the balcony to become refocused. This trip may be for a few minutes or a few days and may involve praying, seeking coaching or counsel, or reading of Scripture. If it serves the reconciliation process, it is worth the trip.

Another aspect to keep in mind as one engages in the reconciliation process is the recognition that people like being compassionately understood, perhaps beyond what they have even understood of themselves. This understanding happens when the listening person suspends a preset point of view and instead reflects back what was heard. The desire to render judgment is lost and understanding the other is paramount. This isn't just parroting back the words said but a reflecting back on the words said, the feelings expressed and the understood meaning or intended message of these words. The reflection may include words like "If I heard you correctly, you said... is this correct?" If it is not understood as the speaker intended, seek clarification until the speaker's position is understood. This does not mean that the listener agrees with the other person's position or understanding of the situation, but in seeking clarification, the speaker will feel connected to the listener. When the listener reflects back the thoughts and feelings of the speaker, the observer part of the speaker gets more activated and feelings are experienced from a new and healthy perspective. The reflections also provide the listener a clearer understanding of the position of the speaker. Value is added to the relationship for both parties, and the possibility of reconciliation increases.

Reflections on Chapter 6

1. Where does prayer fit into the reconciliation process? _____

2. What does one do to mentally prepare for entering the reconciliation process? _____ _____ _____

3. What is the benefit of "building a bridge" to the other person in the reconciliation process? _____ _____ _____

4. List some of the actions of "managing" the reconciliation process. _____ _____ _____

5. Why should a person write down issues/concerns? _____ _____

6. After writing down the issues, what is the next step in the reconciliation process? _____

_____

Why? _____

_____

7. What is a key behavioral component of the actual reconciliation time with the other person? _____

8. If, during the time together of the reconciliation process, either person asks for forgiveness, what is the other person to do? _____

Chapter 7

Forgiveness

Out of the depths I cry to you, O LORD.
> Lord, hear my voice!
Let your ears be attentive
> to the voice of my supplications!

If you, O LORD, should mark iniquities,
> Lord, who could stand?
But there is forgiveness with you,
> so that you may be revered.

I wait for the LORD, my soul waits,
> and in his word I hope;
my soul waits for the Lord
> more than those who watch for the morning,
> more than those who watch for the morning.

O Israel, hope in the LORD!
> For with the LORD there is steadfast love,
> and with him is great power to redeem.
It is he who will redeem Israel
> from all its iniquities. Psa. 130:1-8

> Put away from you all bitterness and wrath and anger and wrangling and slander, together with all malice, and be kind to one another, tenderhearted, forgiving one another, as God in Christ has forgiven you. Eph. 4:31–32 NRSV

This care-fronting reconciliation process opens the door for the other person to be receptive to your concerns. If indeed there was sin in the behavior of the other person that led to your hurt feelings and angry thoughts, and that person confesses and asks for forgiveness, then as a fellow redeemed, you have no choice but to forgive. Jesus made this very clear when he said, "If your brother sins, rebuke him, and if he repents, forgive him. If he sins against you seven times in a day, and seven times comes back to you and says, 'I repent,' forgive him"(Lk. 17:3-4). If there was sin and the other person does not see it or denies that it was sin, forgiveness can still be granted.

That one person should forgive another is easily said, but the operational meaning of that statement is not always understood. Pastors, from the pastoral office and representing Christ, regularly proclaim forgiveness to congregations in worship after they confess their sins. This follows the clear directive from Scripture: "If we claim to be without sin, we deceive ourselves and the truth is not in us. If we confess our sins, he is faithful and just and will forgive us our sins and purify us from all unrighteousness" (1 Jn. 1:8-9). To deny sin is deception of self, but a true heart confession of a sinner to God leads to his seeing the sinner only through the lens of the cross. The obedience of the Son has fully paid for the disobedience of the sinner. We are forgiven. There is new life and hope. There is no binding the sinner to the sins, but there is freedom to live in and through the Gospel. Shame and guilt have been removed, and the soul is filled with new opportunities for servanthood to the Savior. God no longer treats us out of wrath and justice, but through his unending grace, love and mercy.

As important and significant as confession/absolution could and should be in our lives as a component of a worship service it can be easily and quickly overlooked and even dismissed. In some worship services little time and attention is devoted to it. Therefore, it may be seen as unimportant or insignificant. If, on the other hand, ample time is granted, worshipers may get anxious about the time it takes and dismiss it (like an announcement of a ladies aid meeting this Wednesday). Therefore, the sooner it is over, the better. We go through the mechanics of the liturgy or service, but our hearts are in neither the confession nor the spoken absolution.

The implementation of forgiveness into a family may also take on a mechanical process. For example, an eight-year-old brother hits his seven-year-old sister while she is trying to change channels on the TV to watch her program instead of his. Observing the ensuing verbal conflict and the daughter's plea for help, "He hit me!" the father says to his son, "Tell your sister you're sorry." The son mechanically says to his sister, "I'm sorry." The father then directs the attention to his daughter, "Now tell your brother that you forgive him." Just as mechanically as he confessed his sin, she responds, "I forgive you." This may or may not be true confession and absolution, but it is a way to get through the ordeal so that other punishment does not follow. It is an action of obedience and compliance and not necessarily of contrition. In time, this dialogue may grow to have true meaning and be said out of changed, contrite and forgiving hearts, but not at this time.

Forgiveness also may be said through clinched teeth, "I forgive you, but I will never forget!" The words are spoken, but underlying the words are resentment and malice. The mechanics of the forgiveness process are implemented, but true forgiveness is not granted. The heart is still hard. There is still a desire to get even. The speaker still desires retribution and a "pound of flesh."

True forgiveness, on the other hand, is about a changed heart. It is about being the fertile soil in which crops of righteousness are sown, grown and harvested. In explaining the parable of the soils, Jesus said, "But the seed on good soil stands for those with a noble and good heart, who hear the word, retain it, and by persevering produce a crop" (Lk. 8:15). Forgiveness is about a change in us. It is, by God's grace, choosing not to allow that which was said or done to continue to break relationship between us and the other person. It is the letting go of our past so that we can let go of the other person's past and in so doing not be bound to the others nor the other to us. This does not mean that we will cease to hurt. Wounds may run deep and some residual pain may always be there. However, the presence of pain does not mean the absence of forgiveness. A weed in the flower garden does not negate the beauty of the flowers also growing there.

Forgiveness is not pretending that the offense did not really matter. It did. If it did not matter, why would it have such power in affecting thoughts, words and behavior? Rationally trying to deny the impact of an offense only sustains the hurt that leads to the broken relationship. The childhood maxim "Sticks and stones can break my bones but words can never hurt me" may sound bold and courageous, but it may reflect a deeper level of hurt and helplessness. It may be a form of denial to defend against the other person while trying to bolster up one's sense of self-worth. The pain is still there.

Forgiveness is not condoning the behavior of the other. It is not saying that the offensive or sinful behavior is okay. It is not capitulating to a position of acquiescence and saying that things are as they were before the offense. They will never be the same. Each person is different than before the event that broke relationship and neither can go back to the pre-event situation. Infidelity, rape, embezzlement from a church, slanderous email, tweets or text messages, stealing an identity, abusive and offensive behavior may never be forgotten. Therefore, going back as though it never happened is not possible. By the grace of God the relationship may be better than it was before, but it will not be the same.

Forgiveness does not mean that we will forget. Though it is often said that we should forgive and forget, the former is possible, but not necessarily the latter. The memory of a traumatic life-changing event may be always there. What was said or done was said or done, and the memory of it cannot be erased. The offense seems to be embedded in our DNA. It cannot be willed away. Since forgetting is passive and not active, to try intentionally to forget offensive words or actions only make them prominent in our minds.

It may be the case that if we connect forgetting with forgiving, we may pile more guilt upon ourselves. We think that since we still have some memories of the event, we have not truly forgiven the offender. Hence, we may heap false or pseudo guilt upon ourselves and potentially add shame to our self-perception as we see ourselves as a "bad person" for feeling that way. Forgiveness is much more than a memory issue, so we should not put the memory of an event and the forgiveness of it in the same basket.

Many years ago while I was a parish pastor in Michigan, I also served as a chaplain of a township police department. Since it was a small police force, I was able to know the officers, as well as the chief, quite well. The chief was a recovering alcoholic, struggling through a rough marriage that had produced a son who was in prison, serving a life sentence for murder. One day while we were having lunch, he began to reflect on his life as a police officer. In a raspy voice, which came from too many years of smoking and inhaling a pipe, he said, "By the time people are twenty-five years old, they have had enough experiences in their lives that if they told their stories to someone else it would bring tears to their eyes." Since I still remember it, this statement had a strong impact on me. It seems to be so true.

It is probably true of all of us that by the time we have reached the age of twenty-five we have had life-changing, emotionally taxing, negative experiences that will live with us forever. These will never go away nor be forgotten. There may be the abortion that followed a pregnancy due to unprotected sex, and the boy blames the girl for letting it happen. There may be the taking of drugs for the first time and the anger that your best friend gave them to you. There may be the accident in the family car due to your negligence that led to your being denied driving privileges for a year. There may be the convincing of an adult to buy you beer and while driving drunk careening the car off the road into a tree killing one friend while paralyzing another. The list is endless and each person has a story. The question is, can we have experiences that were so distressing and heartbreaking when they happened, and remain so vivid in our memories today, that they will never be forgotten *but* do not bind our present and future lives to them? Can we forgive ourselves as well as others?

By God's grace and through his unconditional love, the answer is yes. As William Meninger wrote in *The Process of Forgiveness*, "Only when we allow our wounds to heal and let forgiveness occur will we free ourselves from our self-imposed prison cells. We forgive them for our own sakes."[5]

Forgiveness is that transformation in self that enables us to be free from self-blame and shame and our need to take revenge on our offender. It is a releasing of our offenders so they are no longer bound to us, and we are no longer bound to them. Richard Foster in *Prayer: Finding the Heart's True Home* states, "Forgiveness means that the power of love that holds us together is greater than the power of the offense that separates us."[6] William Meninger notes that, "Forgiveness is the decision that we have done enough futile hiding, suffering, hating, and fantasizing revenge. It is awareness that the things we have done to ourselves do not affect our offenders, and that we are through hurting ourselves. We are going to stop being the child who 'goes out to eat worms' to get back at her parents."[7] He later states, "Forgiveness is not something we do directly but is something that happens to us. When we stop rubbing salt in our wounds and do whatever is required for it, our wounds will heal."[8] When we allow healing to take place, we will have discovered that forgiveness has taken place. Actually, the memory of the event, once redefined in our minds, may serve as a reminder of the love and grace of God and his power to love us fully, and others, through the ultimate gift of his Son upon the cross.

If during the reconciliation process it becomes evident that the other person did sin but does not acknowledge the sin, then under the umbrella of speaking the truth in love and upon the direction from Jesus, we are called to rebuke or admonish that person (Lk. 17: 3). Out of love, the motive of such action is to bring the one who has missed the mark and trespassed the boundaries of righteous living back to truthfulness. As James wrote, "My brothers, if one of you should wander from the truth and someone should bring him back, remember this: Whoever turns a sinner from the error of his way will save him from death and cover over a multitude of sins" (Ja. 5:19-20). To rebuke another is to admonish another person and to call the behavior what it is, a sin.

Admonishing is not a judgment of personality or character but an impugning or holding another person accountable for that person's behavior in this particular incident. Though the person who committed the sin is a sinner, it is the one piece of behavior that transpired between the two in conflict that is being addressed, *not* everything about that person's life. Only God can see truly into the heart. Therefore, for a person to try to condemn the whole of another person for one event is to move into the realm of playing God. Christ rebuked his own disciples for trying this (Lk. 9:49-50).

An example of such rebuking happened to one of God's anointed. King David, in a moment of weakness, committed adultery with Bathsheba. To cover up the resulting pregnancy, he invited her husband, Uriah, home from a battle, assuming that the long abstinence from his lovely wife would motivate him to want to have sex with her. Instead, "Uriah slept at the entrance to the palace with all his master's servants and did not go down to his house"(2 Sam.11:9). As a man of honor and integrity, he did not feel he should be indulging in sexual activity with his wife when his own men were still out in the battlefield fighting.

In out-of-control reactivity to this action by Uriah, David "wrote a letter to Joab and sent it with Uriah. In it he wrote, 'Put Uriah in the front line where the fighting is fiercest. Then withdraw from him so he will be struck down and die'"(Sam. 11:14-15). As an obedient military officer and faithful to his king, Joab did as he was commanded, and

Uriah was allowed to be killed. David was guilty of idolatry in the forms of jealousy, greed, adultery and murder. His sins were obvious and undeniable.

As an act of love for this morally and ethically fallen servant, the LORD sent Nathan to David to reprove and admonish him for his sins. For his salvation, God used Nathan to rebuke him and bring into light some acts that took place in darkness (2 Sam. 12:1-13). Nathan's approach was to engage David, unemotionally and calmly, in a non-threatening dialog. He did not aggressively attack David through a verbal tirade. Instead, he posed a hypothetical situation and asked for David's counsel.

> The Lord sent Nathan to David. When he came to him, he said, "There were two men in a certain town, one rich and the other poor. The rich man had a very large number of sheep and cattle, but the poor man had nothing but one little ewe lamb he had bought. He raised it, and it grew up with him and his children. It shared his food, drank from his cup and even slept in his arms. It was like a daughter to him.
> Now a traveler came to the rich man, but the rich man refrained from taking one of his own sheep or cattle to prepare a meal for the traveler who had come to him. Instead, he took the ewe lamb that belonged to the poor man and prepared it for the one who had come to him."
> David burned with anger against the man and said to Nathan, "As surly as the LORD lives, the man

who did this deserves to die. He must pay for the lamb four times over, because he did such a thing and had no pity." Then Nathan said to David, "You are the man!"... Then David said to Nathan, "I have sinned against the LORD."

Nathan replied, "The LORD has taken away your sin. You are not going to die" (2 Sam 12:1-13).

By seeking David's advice through a question about truth and justice, Nathan brought David emotionally closer to him. In so doing, David became more transparent and vulnerable to that which was to follow. Nathan had rationally and unemotionally disarmed David and had significantly reduced the potential of his defensiveness and negative reactivity. He tilled the soil so he could plant a seed that would grow. Perhaps because of hearing this story of his father and mother, the very wise Solomon later wrote in the book of Proverbs, "A rebuke strikes deeper in a discerning person than one hundred blows to a fool"(Pr. 17:10). Nathan was helping David become a more discerning person, so he would be more receptive to the admonition that had as its ultimate purpose David's confession of sin and absolution from God.

In a loving manner, Nathan utilized a well-thought-out process to confront perhaps one of the most powerful people in history with his moral and ethical failures. He did not sidestep the issue nor seek to diminish the gravity of David's behavior, but he addressed it in a way that led David to discern for himself the enormity of his own sinful behavior.

As a result of Nathan's story and his being a follower of the living and forgiving God, David recognized the need to take ownership of his own sinful behavior and confess it to his Lord, who forgave him. His response to the rebuke was not to attack the one who rebuked him but to see the benefit of what the rebuke had done for him in calling him to accountability. The rebuke allowed him to humble himself, to "come clean," and to no longer have his past haunt his present and future. We should learn from Nathan's wisdom and David's humility how to rebuke and how to respond to it.

David never forgot the depth or gravity of the sins he committed. Instead, he recognized the need to confess his sins and in so doing also recognized that the God who blessed him with many gifts and called him into the leadership position as king, also forgave him for his grievous acts against man and God. As David carried the story of his sins, he, more importantly, carried the reality that the love of God is stronger than any act of mankind, regardless of how disgraceful and shameful it may be. As the apostle Paul later wrote, "where sin increased, grace increased all the more" (Rom. 5:20).

Reflections on Chapter 7

1. Can true forgiveness be feigned? _____ If not, what does it take for true forgiveness? _____
_____

2. Is it true that to truly forgive one must forget? _____
Why not? _____
_____
_____

3. Describe some aspects of true forgiveness. _____
_____
_____

4. In the story about David, Bathsheba, Uriah and Nathan,
   a. What is learned about God in dealing with sin?
_____
_____
_____
_____

b. What is learned about how to respond if we are confronted with our sin (s)? _____
_____
_____
_____

c. May there be consequences to our sinful behavior even if we are forgiven? ___ Explain your answer. _____
_____
_____

Chapter 8

Closing Thoughts

Inasmuch as the desire for the reconciliation process is the state of being reconciled, this does not mean that one attempt at it will produce the desired outcome. The process may break down in any number of ways and for a variety of reasons. A detailed reading of chapters 18-26 of 1 Samuel reveals an interesting story. Saul was the first God-appointed king of Israel. David, his successor, was probably the greatest king of Israel. David's reign began before Saul died. Due to a variety of reasons, Saul was always envious of David and at one point actually tried to kill him (1 Sam. 19:1-10). In spite of Saul's aggressiveness toward him, David always respected Saul and continuously sought to reconcile with him.

Each time David tried, Saul rebuffed him. It seemed to be a fruitless effort, but David never gave up. He even had many opportunities to kill Saul and just end the whole matter, but out of respect for this called servant of God (fourth-level values), David could not and would not. After their last dialogue (1 Sam. 26:25), they parted ways. David, along with all of his family and six hundred soldiers fled to Gath, and Saul no longer sought him (1 Sam. 27:4). From what we read in Scripture, reconciliation between these two great men of God never took place.

Reconciliation between people takes a commitment by both parties to want to reconcile. First, the process has to be entered into "in good faith" by both parties. Second, it takes time. It cannot be rushed. Third, it takes a changed heart by both parties. The hearts that initially entered into the conflict cannot be the hearts that will lead to a reconciled relationship. It is only through transformed and renewed hearts that reconciliation can take place. Since hearts are changed by the Spirit that blows as it wills through a variety of means, including his Word, the Sacraments, prayer, encounters with others and even the reconciliation process itself, it is never known when healing will take place. However, as healing takes place in the hearts of both, the reconciliation process will move forward.

Some suggested passages for further reading:

Mt. 6:12-15
> Forgive us our debts, as we also have forgiven our debtors. And lead us not into temptation, but deliver us from the evil one. For if you forgive men when they sin against you, your heavenly Father will also forgive you. But if you do not forgive men their sins, your Father will not forgive your sins.

Eph. 4:29-32
> Do not let any unwholesome talk come out of your mouths, but only what is helpful for building others up according to their needs, that it may benefit those who listen. And do not grieve the Holy Spirit of God, with whom you were sealed for the day of redemption. Get rid of all bitterness, rage and anger, brawling and slander, along with every form of malice. Be kind and compassionate to one another, forgiving each other, just as in Christ God forgave you.

Phil. 2:1-16
> If you have any encouragement from being united with Christ, if any comfort from his love, if any fellowship with the Spirit, if any tenderness and compassion, then make my joy complete by being like-minded, having the same love, being one in spirit and purpose. Do nothing out of selfish ambition or vain conceit, but in humility consider others better than yourselves. Each of you should look not only to your own interests, but also to the interests of others. Your attitude should be the same as that of

Christ Jesus: Who, being in very nature God, did not consider equality with God something to be grasped, but made himself nothing, taking the very nature of a servant, being made in human likeness. And being found in appearance as a man, he humbled himself and became obedient to death — even death on a cross! Therefore God exalted him to the highest place and gave him the name that is above every name, that at the name of Jesus every knee should bow, in heaven and on earth and under the earth, and every tongue confess that Jesus Christ is Lord, to the glory of God the Father.

Therefore, my dear friends, as you have always obeyed — not only in my presence, but now much more in my absence — continue to work out your salvation with fear and trembling, for it is God who works in you to will and to act according to his good purpose.

Do everything without complaining or arguing, so that you may become blameless and pure, children of God without fault in a crooked and depraved generation, in which you shine like stars in the universe as you hold out the word of life.

Col. 3:12-16
> Therefore, as God's chosen people, holy and dearly loved, clothe yourselves with compassion, kindness, humility, gentleness and patience. Bear with each other and forgive whatever grievances you may have against one another. Forgive as the Lord forgave you. And over all these virtues put on love, which binds them all together in perfect unity.

Let the peace of Christ rule in your hearts, since as members of one body you were called to peace. And be thankful. Let the word of Christ dwell in you richly as you teach and admonish one another with all wisdom, and as you sing psalms, hymns and spiritual songs with gratitude in your hearts to God.

Some guiding principles

1. When the reconciliation process is completed, the other will have seen Christ in me.

2. The process will be entered into in good faith that God's will, not mine, will be done.

3. Needs and interests, as well as problems and positions, will be expressed.

4. If I have sinned, I will confess my sin and ask for forgiveness.

5. That without reservation, if the other has sinned and has asked for forgiveness, I will forgive.

6. That within the boundaries of Christian love, grace and mercy, I will seek to bring about a reconciliation that is God-pleasing.

7. That if a sense of brokenness continues after the meeting time of the process, I will continue to discern my part in the brokenness and seek to move toward personal health and wholeness as a member of the body of Christ.

Endnotes

---

[1] Oswald Chambers, *My Utmost for His Highest* (Uhrichsville, Ohio: Barbour, 1935) 63.

[2] Ronald A. Heifetz and Marty Linsky, *Leadership on the Line* (Boston: Harvard Business School Press, 2002), 51.

[3] Ibid.

[4] David Augsburger, *Caring Enough to Confront* (Scottdale, Pennsylvania: Herald Press, 1973), 10.

[5] William A. Menninger, *The Process of Forgiveness* (New York: Continuum, 2001), 27.

[6] Richard Foster, *Prayer: Finding the Heart's True Home* (San Francisco: Harper, 1992), 188.

[7] Menninger, *The Process*, 35.

[8] Ibid. 37.

Bibliography

Amen, Daniel G. *Change Your Brain Change Your Life*. New York: Random House, 1998.

Augsburger, David. *Caring Enough to Confront*. Scottdale, Pennsylvania: Herald Press, 1973.

Bowen, Murray. *Family Therapy in Clinical Practice*. Northvale: Jason Aronson, 1994.

Bregman, Ona Cohn and Charles M. White. *Bringing Systems Thinking to Life*. New York: Routledge, 2011.

Chambers, Oswald. *My Utmost for His Highest*. Uhrichsville, Ohio: Barbour, 1935.

Cloud, Henry and John Townsend. *Boundaries*. Grand Rapids, Michigan: Zondervan Publishing House, 1995.

Concordia Study Bible. St. Louis: Concordia Publishing House, 1986.

Fine, Cordella. *A Mind of Its Own*. New York: W.W. Norton & Company, 2006.

Foster, Richard J. *Prayer: Finding the Heart's True Home*. San Francisco: Harper, 1992.

Friedman, Edwin H. *Generation to Generation: Family Process in Church and Synogogue*. New York: The Guilford Press, 1985.

Gilbert, Roberta M. *The Eight Concepts of Bowen Theory*. Falls Church & Basye, Virginia: Leading Systems Press, 2004.

Gilbert, Roberta M. *Extraordinary Leadership*. Falls Church & Basye, Virginia: Leading Systems Press, 2006.

Greenleaf, Robert K. *The Power of Servant Leadership*. San Francisco: Berrett-Koehler Publishers, 1998.

Heifetz, Ronald A. and Marty Linsky. *Leadership on the Line*. Boston: Harvard Business School Press, 2002.

Hirsch, John M. "Pastoral Leadership in Dysfunctional Congregations: A Family Systems Approach Toward Wholeness". Unpublished doctoral dissertation, Western Theological Seminary, Holland, Michigan, 1998.

Isay, Dave. *Listening Is an Act of Love*. New York: The Penguin Press, 2007.

Kolb, Robert and Timothy J. Wengert, Eds. *The Book of Concord*. Minneapolis: Fortress Press, 2000.

Leman, Kevin. *The New Birth Order Book*. Grand Rapids: Fleming H. Revell, 1998.

McIntosch, Gary L. and Samuel D. Rima. *Overcoming the Dark Side of Leadership*. Grand Rapids: Baker Books, 2001.

Menninger, William A. *The Process of Forgiveness*. New York: Continuum, 2001.

Ortberg, John. *God is Closer Than You Think*. Grand Rapids: Zondervan, 2005.

Pargament, Kenneth I. *The Psychology of Religion and Coping*. New York: The Guilford Press, 1997.

Qualben, James. *Peace in the Parish*. San Antonio: Langmarc Publishing, 1991.

Restack, Richard. *The Brain Has a Mind of Its Own*. New York: Crown Trade Paperbacks, 1991.

Restack, Richard. *The New Brain: How the Modern Age Is Rewiring Your Mind*. Rodale, 2003.

Richardson, Ronald W. *Creating a Healthier Church*. Minneapolis: Fortress Press, 1996.

Sande, Ken. *The Peacemaker*. Grand Rapids: Baker Books, 1997.

Sandford, John A. *Evil: The Shadow Side of Reality.* New York: Crossroad Publishing Company, 2001.

Sawyer, David R. *Hope in Conflict: Discovering Wisdom in Congregational Turmoil.* Cleveland: Pilgrim Press, 2007.

Steinke, Peter L. *Congregational Leadership in Anxious Times.* Herndon: The Alban Institute, 2006.

Steinke, Peter L. *A Door Set Open.* Herndon, Virginia: The Alban Institute, 2010.

Steinke, Peter L. *Healthy Congregations: a systems approach.* An Alban Institute Publication, 1996.

Steinke, Peter L. *How Your Church Family Works.* An Alban Institute Publication, 1993.

CPSIA information can be obtained at www.ICGtesting.com
Printed in the USA
LVOW111840150412

277647LV00001B/3/P